T0306028

Future Normal

This is a book for leaders who think about legacy, their own and the one their business is leaving. Yet, none of us get to write our legacy, that is for those who come after us. This book and the lessons within will enable you to improve yours.

The eight questions at the core of this book are underpinned by three big ideas:

1   The questions we ask matter.
2   Businesses are the tools we use to shape our world.
3   Business value is optimized for the long term when society thrives.

The questions have been developed and road-tested with business leaders and thousands of executives on an MBA that is ranked number one in the world as 'best for the planet'. Applying them to your business will enable long-term value creation while shifting it to one that your children will be proud of.

This book will appeal to business executives, leaders and managers, MBA graduates and students, and all those interested in transforming their organizations for the challenges ahead.

Nick Barter is Professor of Strategy and Sustainability at Griffith Business School. Completing his doctorate at the University of St Andrews, his career has spanned industry and academia, from strategy consulting with EY to advising executives on escaping myopic strategic thinking, to leading the Griffith MBA.

Christopher Fleming is Professor of Economics and Dean (Research) at the Griffith Business School. Completing his doctorate at the University of Queensland, his career has spanned the public sector, academia leading the Griffith MBA, and industry providing advice on economic frameworks that align with our lived reality.

NICK BARTER AND
CHRISTOPHER FLEMING

Future Normal
8 Questions to Create
Businesses Your Children
will be Proud Of

Routledge
Taylor & Francis Group

LONDON AND NEW YORK

Designed cover image by Erika Gumaru

First published 2024
by Routledge
4 Park Square, Milton Park, Abingdon, Oxon, OX14 4RN

and by Routledge
605 Third Avenue, New York, NY 10158

Routledge is an imprint of the Taylor & Francis Group, an informa business

© 2023 Nick Barter and Christopher Fleming

British Library Cataloguing-in-Publication Data
A catalogue record for this book is available from the British Library

Library of Congress Cataloging-in-Publication Data
Names: Barter, Nick, author. | Fleming, Christopher (Christopher M.), author.
Title: Future normal : 8 questions to create businesses your children will
be proud of / Nick Barter and Christopher Fleming.
Description: Abingdon, Oxon ; New York, NY : Routledge, 2024. |
Includes bibliographical references. |
Identifiers: LCCN 2023025201 (print) | LCCN 2023025202 (ebook) |
ISBN 9781032419756 (hardback) | ISBN 9781032419749 (paperback) |
ISBN 9781003360636 (ebook)
Subjects: LCSH: Social responsibility of business. | Business ethics.
Classification: LCC HD60 .B386 2024 (print) |
LCC HD60 (ebook) | DDC 658.4/08–dc23/eng/20230721
LC record available at https://lccn.loc.gov/2023025201
LC ebook record available at https://lccn.loc.gov/2023025202

ISBN: 9781032419756 (hbk)
ISBN: 9781032419749 (pbk)
ISBN: 9781003360636 (ebk)

DOI: 10.4324/9781003360636

Typeset in Joanna MT
by Newgen Publishing UK

Contents

Figures

Abbreviations

ESG	Environmental, Social and Governance
GDP	Gross Domestic Product
GNP	Gross National Product
HDI	Human Development Index
INO	Inclusion of Nature in Organization
INS	Inclusion of Nature in Self
IPCC	Intergovernmental Panel on Climate Change
OECD	Organization for Economic Cooperation and Development
PPM	Parts Per Million
SDGs	Sustainable Development Goals
UN	United Nations
USA	United States of America
UK	United Kingdom

Acknowledgement of Country

This book was written on the traditional lands of the Yugarabul, Yuggera, Jagera, Turrbal and Gubbi Gubbi peoples. We acknowledge the traditional owners and custodians of the lands on which we live and work and pay our respects to Elders, past, present and future, and extend that respect to all Aboriginal and Torres Strait Islander people. We recognise sovereignty was never ceded and that the land that is Australia was founded on the genocide and dispossession of First Nations people. We acknowledge that colonial structures are still in place and as such the struggles of First Nations peoples continue. The wounds that have lasted for generations will perpetuate forward and not heal unless we engage in ongoing listening and discussion with those who have been and still are so harmed. The process of full healing will take generations and we support all efforts to achieve justice, recognition and respect for all First Nations people. We humbly receive their advice and guidance on how to realize such outcomes so that we can all move together into a better future.

We were lucky enough to be born in countries that allowed us to study and have freedom of thought. We both won a form of lottery with such a start. We are also both middle aged, white, male professors. The clichés abound. The wind has been at our backs all our lives and we hope the future erodes such privileges to lift others. Further, we recognise the privilege that has swept us along and picked us up when it would have and has trampled others and we recognise the injustices upon which our privilege was built. The privilege we have as white males has been built off the back of others especially people of colour, but also women and so many others that have been marginalized. We would like to acknowledge them; their sacrifice and we hope our work is helping in some small way to right previous wrongs. More specifically, given we are based in Australia, it is very important to us that the beauty of the land upon which we live, and which constitutes us is acknowledged and that we respect the human history of this land, a land that has a human story that dates back 60,000 years or more.

To close, we would like to offer some specific acknowledgements to those who have helped with the book, the team at Routledge in Singapore and John Tague from the Griffith Review, and to those closest to us, our wives Shona and Michelle, our children Grace, Morran and Thomas, our extended families and friends. We are, because you are.

Thank you for picking up this book. It is a book for leaders who think about legacy, their own and the one their business is leaving. If this opening sentence hasn't grabbed you and you are about to put the book down, before you do, use your phone to take a picture of the contents page. On that page you will see eight questions. We urge you to spend some time reflecting on these questions, as we believe they can significantly shape the future of your business for the better. If, however, we have piqued your curiosity, please read on.

   This book, like all books, is caught between narratives. One narrative concerns why the book was written (the story outside the covers), another the narrative that exists between the covers (the one you will hopefully read), and then there is a narrative that results from you having read the book (the story you will tell). This preface is an attempt to explain why this book was written. The simple answer is that we would like business leaders to be more ambitious. We would like them to view their businesses not as ends in and of themselves, but as tools that can enable great outcomes for all. We may well be in an era where some of our most clement times are behind us. The forecasts of the future, which science has enabled, indicate that those who come after us are going to face significant challenges. This is not a good gift to pass to the next generation, especially when many of us consider ourselves as leaders who want to leave a positive legacy. Hence, there is a need to do things differently. At the core of this book are eight questions that, in our view, are necessary to enable your business to start shifting towards the Future Normal, a future where businesses act meaningfully in their surroundings and purposefully to benefit themselves and society.

As you note the questions, they may appear to you as *now radical*. Our contention is that they will become Future Normal. History indicates that the now radical has always been a portend to the Future Normal, be it those once radical movements that helped create paid holiday leave, or a forty-hour working week, or health and safety measures in the work-place. Or the once radical movements that agitated for a woman's right to vote, equal pay, gay marriage, civil rights and so forth. Our Future Normal depends on the now radical.

We also have a window into the Future Normal through the conversations we have with the next generation, the generation that will be running the world in thirty years' time. The next generation are concerned about the future of our societies and our surroundings, they want what we all want – decent work, a healthy free and fair society, clean air, clean water and abundant wildlife. These are simple asks, yet somehow such enduring and simple asks are being lost. We propose that some of the blame for this lies with the conventional theories of business that haunt us. This book will try and unravel some of those.

If you are still a little unsure about pressing on and continuing to read, perhaps consider what we call the 'Greta Thunberg test'. We note some individuals react badly to Greta. If you are one such individual, please don't, Greta is a key cipher to understanding the views of the next gen-eration of leaders. She offers you and all business leaders a window into the thinking of the younger generation. These windows are openings for strategy development. Thus, no matter whether you like or dislike her messages, they point to your legacy as a leader and how the younger generation will judge it. As you know, your rating as a leader is not made by you, it is made by those that come after.

Thus, the Greta Thunberg test is this: imagine you are sitting across the table from the younger generation, perhaps your children, and they are asking you questions about the business you lead and if it is per-petuating better outcomes over the coming decades. In your mind, how are you answering such questions, what score would you give yourself? What score would they give you? Having used your imagination, per-haps try the test in real life. Our experience indicates too many leaders fail the test; they are placing a debt on those that follow. This is not a good legacy and we can do better.

Hence, this book is a guide for you, it is your cheat sheet to getting a great test score and leaving a positive legacy while creating long term value for your business. Embracing the eight questions at the core of this book will shift your business towards it becoming one that your children will be proud of and one that has optimal value over the long term. The questions have been developed over decades of consulting, advising and teaching. They have been road-tested with business leaders and thousands of executives on an MBA that is ranked number one in the world as "best for the planet".[1]

So, the why of this book: to help you create change. The focus is on you because businesses are the tools we use to shape our world, and those that lead them, people such as yourself, can effect significant change and leave a legacy that future generations will thank you for ... or not. The choice is yours.

Before closing, a personal side bar. This book has been in the back of our minds for many years. In the late 1990s when Nick was working in a strategy consultancy in the UK and Chris in sustainable development policy in New Zealand. At this time, one of the crowning edifices of Western business thought was encapsulated in a phrase uttered by Gordon Gekko, a character in the 1987 film *Wall Street*. The phrase was "greed is good". A great meme for sure, but not a fundamental truth. Such a statement didn't ring true to us then and still doesn't. As this book reveals, economists and corporate strategists have spent decades trying to make such a statement truth. However, such thinking is misplaced, limiting our ambition and hampering our ability to prosper in the long term. Highlighting the fallacy of such thinking, however, is not a message always well received, and we have had to build our case through time to be able to publish this book. For example, in the late 1990s, Nick the strategy consultant took to the whiteboard with the consultancy partners in the room and attempted to highlight the fallacy of such thinking. He highlighted how only thinking in money closed options for strategic foresight, as the right answers are always found in making one number bigger than the other, revenue up, costs down, an absurdly simplistic foundation upon which to build meaningful business strategies. The response to this was underwhelming, bringing with it the realization that some of us do not like illusions to be dispelled. Coming to the present, this book unpacks these illusions, reinforces fundamentals and in turn challenges what we view as a paucity of ambition in business leaders.

To close, prior to you turning the page and beginning a journey of innovation, challenge and curiosity, the most important question to leave you with, not included in the eight, yet implicit in them all, is: what type of world is your business perpetuating? Pondering this question will reveal insights about your business that will be the seeds of more adventurous strategies. You could stop here, put the book down and save yourself some time and money. However, if you have made it this far, press on. We think business is one of the most fun things you can do. The decisions and actions you take as a leader impact so much of our world. You will have even more fun if you fully embrace shifting your business to one that acts meaningfully in our surroundings and purposefully to benefit itself and society – *Future Normal* (www.futurenormal.net).

NOTE

1 Since 2010, sustainable-economy media and research organization Corporate Knights has ranked MBA programs according to those that best equip graduates to change the world for the better. Griffith Business School's MBA program first entered the ranking in 2017, coming in 16th place. The program moved into the top five in 2018 and 2019. In 2020, 2021 and 2022 the program was ranked number one in the world, the only MBA program to have achieved this accolade three times. See: https://www.corporateknights.com/rankings/top-40-mba-rankings/.

PART I

Every strategy starts with a question. When that question is asked with curiosity, the space for innovation is created, giving you permission to consider new opportunities and make bolder strategic moves. This is the first big idea of this book. *The questions we ask, and how we ask them, matters.* If this book achieves what we hope it will, your business will be able to shift from strategies that are rooted in last century thinking towards new approaches that enable all stakeholders to thrive now and into the future. To help you begin this shift, this book contains eight questions designed to push boundaries. This book will not give you all the answers, however it will give you the tools to spark the conversations that begin your businesses' journey towards its Future Normal, which we define as being a business that acts meaningfully in its surroundings[1] and purposefully to benefit itself and society.

We are at a point in time where the purpose of business needs to be redefined. For too many decades business theory and conventional business narratives have aided and abetted the simplification of the purpose of business to answering a single question: How do we maximize profit? This question constrains leaders into looking at their organization primarily through a monetary lens. This reduces the challenge of leading an organization to a simple algorithm, selling goods or services for more than they cost, making one number (revenue) larger than another (costs). The problem with this reduction is that a wider perspective is lost and any meaningful consideration of how a strategy impacts your business' long-term value, society and our surroundings is ignored.

DOI: 10.4324/9781003360636-2

This monetary lens is fraying at the edges and has lost its legitimacy. Consider for a moment the behaviors a singular focus on profit maximization permits, or even encourages. On the revenue side, history is awash with examples of questionable strategies employed to maintain or enhance revenue, ranging from tobacco companies deliberately sowing doubt on the science linking cigarette smoking to lung cancer,[2] to subprime lending in the lead up to the 2007–08 global financial crisis.[3] On the cost side, cost minimization, despite being given the virtuous sounding moniker 'productive efficiency' in economic theory, promotes behaviors such as paying workers as little as possible, seeking inputs as cheaply as possible (ignoring, for example, the environmental damage of unsustainable natural resource extraction or the human costs of sweatshop labor) and disposing of waste at as low cost as possible, which often means directly into our surroundings with little pretreatment, polluting the water we drink and the air we breathe. In short, an unrelenting and narrow focus on profit maximization has made it harder for us to thrive.

Consequently, a shift is starting to emerge where more is expected of businesses and their leaders.[4] Expecting more requires a move from the simple to the complex. We can no longer consider businesses as money making machines operating to a single algorithm of revenue versus cost, separate from where and how we live (the simple). Rather, we need to recognize that *businesses are the tools we use to shape society and our surroundings* (the complex); this is the second big idea of this book. That is, businesses are tools of change that are constituted by us, they are enacted through our behavior and their strategies are realized through the questions we ask; our organizations shape us, and we shape them.

It should be noted that this more complex view is not about sacrificing profits, it is about understanding that money is not made in isolation from society, rather it is made as an outcome of exchanges between people who make up our society. Thus, *business value is optimized when society thrives*; this is the third big idea.

The aim of this book is to help you develop strategies to lead your organization to optimal value, strategies underpinned by three ideas:

1   The questions we ask, and how we ask them, matters.
2   Businesses are the tools we use to shape society and our surroundings.
3   Business value is optimized when society thrives.

Embracing these ideas will enable you to lead your organization to become Future Normal.

The content of this book is ambitious and optimistic. It is challenging, as it asks you to reflect and consider how your organization is operating and whether it is helping create a world you would like those that come after you, your children, to live in. In this context, the book provides an opportunity for the strategic direction and organizational development of your business to be much more adventurous and more rewarding.

This book is about you not being trapped by the past, by convention or inheritance, rather it is forward facing and about you leading an organization that is enabling a more prosperous society for those that come after us. Thus, the approach is about enabling future prosperity and as such it is aligned, but not reducible, to the arguments contained within the sustainable development agenda. The key difference is that where sustainable development can be defined as "…development that meets the needs of the present without compromising the ability of future generations to meet their own needs",[5] the Future Normal approach goes further, it is about *improving* the ability of future generations to meet their needs. Noting that a generation is a period of 30 years, a timescale we can all imagine. Thus, the next 'future' generation are not unknowable individuals yet to be born, rather they are thirty years younger than yourself: you know some of them, you can talk to them, they may even be your children. Consequently, looking after future generations is not some imaginary exercise, rather it is about speaking to those younger than us and considering their views.

Turning to the book's structure, it opens by highlighting how history haunts our present and limits strategic possibilities. From there, Chapter 3 develops an understanding of how we should consider our organizations as conversations in all facets of their operations. The following eight chapters present the questions we urge you to ask of your organization. Each chapter outlines a question, the rationale for asking it, its underpinning theory or theories, some examples to help illuminate and some discussion of how you can make a start in your business. In this way, each chapter provides both theory and advice on application. Chapter 12, the final chapter, summarizes the key arguments and offers guidance on next steps.

Focusing on the eight questions, they have been designed to collapse any psychological distance as conventional business language tends towards abstraction and separation, creating a fallacy of separation whereby organizations are discussed as something operating separately and apart from our surroundings and societies.[6] This is not the world we live in, and such a fallacy is a cognitive trap this book aims to avoid. As such, the questions are not phrased in a manner that objectifies and separates. Rather, they are questions that put you and your business at the center of the action. The rationale for this form of questioning is to ensure we all deal in the idea that businesses are not free floating from our society, but rather are tools we use to shape our future and are informed by our attitudes, beliefs and the questions we ask.

To highlight this, the first question explores whether your organization has a vision that perpetuates a world you want to live in. Thus, it is a question that is focused on the strategic direction of your business. The second concerns cultural alignment within the business, within a frame of understanding the human/nature relationship, as we will not realize more prosperous societies if the culture of your organization is one that separates humans from the world around us. The third question explores stakeholders and who or what you and your business listen to, noting that many businesses are very selective in their hearing. The fourth explores measures, as without measurement little is realized. The fifth explores language and the role of metaphor and psychological distance. The sixth explores business footprints, as to enable more sustainable outcomes your business needs to know how hard it is treading and what can be done to reduce this. The seventh explores parameters for innovation in production and consumption, and whether innovation can be inspired by the systems that surround us. The final question explores shifting from a zero-sum paranoid focus on competition to a perspective of leading by enabling others. Taken together, the questions within this book serve as a key enabler of change for your organization. They will provide you with the ability to create new strategies; strategies that will enhance your business' value in the coming decades.

To close, this book will give you the confidence to lead in a more purposeful way.

NOTES

1 While the term 'environment' will at times appear in this book, we prefer to use the term 'surroundings' to describe the world around us. The challenge with the term environment is that it has echoes of separatist categorical thinking that we need to move past; we tend to create a distance between ourselves and the environment, thinking that the environment is some separate space. Surroundings on the other hand tends to collapse this distance.

2 *Merchants of Doubt* is an excellent 2010 book written by Naomi Oreskes and Erik Conway describing the strategies many industries, including the tobacco industry, have used to try and undermine scientific research to protect their business models. Oreskes, N., & Conway, E.M. (2011). *Merchants of Doubt: How a Handful of Scientists Obscured the Truth on Issues from Tobacco Smoke to Global Warming.* Bloomsbury Publishing USA. For more information about tobacco industry strategies, including strategies still being employed today, see https://tobaccotactics.org/, a platform for dissemination of academic research maintained by the University of Bath's Tobacco Control Research Group.

3 A short essay on the origins of the subprime mortgage crisis can be found on the US Federal Reserve History website. See: https://www.federalreservehistory.org/essays/subprime-mortgage-crisis.

4 See the Edelman Trust Barometer for an understanding of how society now expects businesses to take a lead in solving societal challenges: https://www.edelman.com/trust.

5 This is the most widely accepted definition of sustainable development and can be found in the United Nations *Report of the World Commission on Environment and Development: Our Common Future*, also known as the Brundtland Report after Gro Harlem Brundtland, who was chairperson of the World Commission at the time. The full text of the report is provided here: https://sustainabledevelopment.un.org/content/documents/5987 our-common-future.pdf. The definition of sustainable development is at the beginning of section IV.

6 In 2013 Nick and a colleague Sally Russell, Professor and Chair of Sustainability and Organisational Behaviour in the School of Earth and Environment at the University of Leeds, published an article examining the dominance of machine and organism metaphors in organizational studies. In this article they argue that these metaphors impede progress towards sustainable development because they perpetuate a story that dehumanizes and de-prioritizes humans at the expense of the organization, which in turn becomes a rarefied and prioritized subject. As an alternative, they offer the metaphor of the organization as a tool, which leads to the second big idea of this book – that businesses are the tools we use to shape society and our surroundings. See: Barter, N., & Russell, S. (2013). Organisational metaphors and sustainable development: Enabling or inhibiting? *Sustainability Accounting, Management and Policy Journal*, 4(2), 145-162. https://doi.org/10.1108/SAMPJ-Jan-2012-0002.

Two

Every review of a current situation, be it personal or professional, involves a reflection on how we've come to be where we are. Such assessments involve examining the decisions and assumptions that have led us to the present point. In this vein, when conventional approaches prove to be inadequate, it is a sign that old thinking and old theories are fraying. The path that brought us to the now and the assumptions and decisions within that path are not ones that will lead to desired outcomes in the future. When faced with such a situation, a natural tendency can be to cling to the comfort of convention. This shows itself by businesses clinging to the old ways; perhaps continuing to offer a product or service that has served it well for decades, rather than beginning a transition to the new. In this way, history can haunt the present and be an obstacle to, rather than an enabler of change.

A prescient example of this are oil companies, which are still profiting from the burning of fossil fuels. They have reinforced their conventional business model and attempted to delay the onset of the new through a concerted campaign of obfuscation about the challenges of climate change.[1] It is worth noting that the underlying science of climate change was understood almost 200 years ago[2] and in 1988 the United Nations established the IPCC (Intergovernmental Panel on Climate Change) to help us monitor, better understand and respond. However, in the more than 30 years since the IPCC's establishment, our inability to accept the rationality and implications of the science has meant that emissions have increased by over 50 percent.[3]

The question then arises as to why this is the case, why do organizations, such as oil companies, stay wedded to their conventions?

DOI: 10.4324/9781003360636-3

Why does history haunt the present and hinder the emergence of the new? The answer found in the popular press is invariably short-term greed. This is undoubtedly a factor – however, in our view, there is a more profound explanation.

All of us live in the eternal present moment and draw on lessons from the past to inform our next move. The challenge for leaders is that the truth of the past can become so engrained that they lack the mental flexibility, and crucially the will, to change. This is understandable as few people like change. It takes effort to obtain new understanding and engrain new habits. Given this, leaders frequently seek to maintain historical truths, as to deny them would mean challenging the truths of their career, the truths that enabled them to prosper. This may impact their very sense of self, especially as the personal purpose of leaders is often bound up in the strategy of the organization.[4] Hence, history haunts our present because change takes effort, and individuals couple their sense of self too closely to their history.

This lack of flexibility, however, is odd, as being open to change when new evidence emerges is a key indicator of an entrepreneurial mindset. The irony is that businesses continually press for thinking 'outside the box', and every established industry of the now was once new, innovative and led by individuals with the mental flexibility to challenge convention.

The aims of this chapter are twofold. The first is to offer a macro-level view of our changing context and introduce a thought experiment to underline how a changing context can push us to consider a change in strategies. The second is to highlight a history of conventional business thinking and its associated fallacies. As such, Figure 2.1 contains two key elements, the first is the population of our planet and the carbon dioxide parts per million (ppm) in our atmosphere through time. The second is a timeline highlighting key developments in business theory as well as some countervailing views. Please note that the timeline offered in Figure 2.1 is *a* timeline, as opposed to *the* timeline; it is schematic, as opposed to a detailed truth.

A CHANGING CONTEXT

Referring to Figure 2.1 and the dark grey boxes, they start in the year 1850 and end in 2050, each highlighting the global human population and the global atmospheric carbon dioxide concentration in that year, noting that the population and ppm for 2050 are not yet known. Rapid growth in the

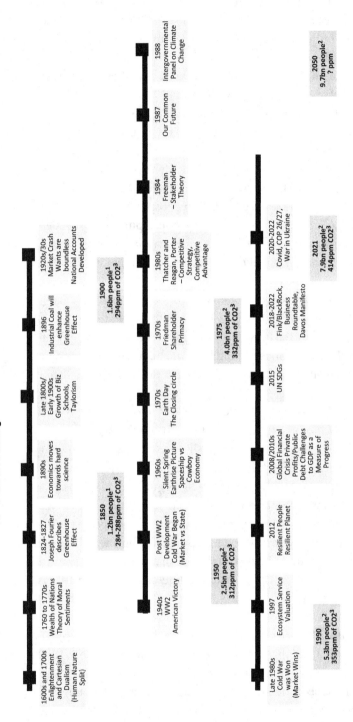

Figure 2.1 A timeline, not the timeline

1 – Pre 1950 estimates from https://en.wikipedia.org/wiki/Estimates_of_historical_world_population – UNESA estimates.

2 – Post 1950 estimates from the United Nations Data Portal – https://population.un.org/dataportal/data/indicators/49/locations/900/start/1950/end/2100/line/linetimeplot.

3 – EPA – Environmental Protection Agency – Global Atmospheric Concentrations of Carbon Dioxide over time – Available from https://www.epa.gov/climate-indicators/climate-change-indicators-atmospheric-concentrations-greenhouse-gases.

global population between 1850 to 2021 is evident, a sixfold increase. More starkly, since 1950, just seventy-two years ago relative to 2022, the global population has more than tripled, reaching eight billion on 15 November 2022.[5] This growth has occurred on one planet, a planet that is materially closed and energy open.[6]

To explore this changing context further, it is useful to engage in a thought experiment. Consider the room you are currently in as the Earth. Between 1950 and 2022 the number of people in the room has tripled, yet the size of the room has not changed. If you are reading this in a room alone, imagine the room with three people rather than one. Similarly, the amount of material contained within the room has not changed but it has been rearranged to suit our desires. Thinking of the Earth, we have felled forests, fished oceans and mined rocks to help fuel and build our modern societies. This rearranging is ongoing, and it is changing the possibilities of what people in the room can do. Individuals who arrived in the room after the first are evermore constricted in what they can do given the rearrangement that the first individual has conducted. When there is one person in the room, if that individual is a smoker of cigarettes there is little concern, likewise what they eat, drink and do with their waste. The room is big enough to handle one person's patterns of behavior, it can provide the inputs and deal with the outputs. However, when there are three people in the room the rules may need to change. For example, the second and third person may not be smokers and as such they might talk to the smoker about filtering the smoke, so it is not harmful and does not impact the air they all breathe. Likewise, they might discuss whether to plant extra trees to offset the emissions from the smoking or whether the waste of the cigarettes should be recycled, as opposed to piling it up in the corner, never completely out of sight and certainly not 'away'.[7] It is obvious that as more people share the room, the pursuit of individual outcomes may not need to be stopped, but the means of production and treatment of waste may need to be re-evaluated, as an increasing population puts different logics in place regarding optimal strategies and operating conditions for all.

Building on this, since 1950 to 2022, the global atmospheric concentration of carbon dioxide has increased by a third and, simplistically, our room is warmer. Parts of the room are becoming less habitable, and the time is coming where the room's inhabitants will seek to move to those areas that are cooler. Further, the systems in the room that provide the air we breathe, the food we eat and the water we drink are showing signs of stress. In short, the context is changing, reinforcing that what might have worked for one will not be as manageable for three. The logical response is to develop a new set of strategies to enable our prosperity into the future, particularly because predictions indicate that there could be another person in the room by 2050 and the aim is that all four people thrive.

As you consider this thought experiment, some key lessons arise. The first is that a changing context implies that strategies appropriate in the past may no longer be appropriate for the present, let alone the future. A second, less obvious, lesson is that you likely approached the thought experiment from a Rawlsian perspective.[8] That is, you did not consider who the others in the room were, specifically you did not think about them in terms of their gender, where they were born, the color of their skin, their wealth or social status. Rather, it is likely your concern was that all thrive and have equal opportunity. The third is that with the potential arrival of a fourth person in 2050, you likely assumed that they should have as much opportunity as the existing three. Thus, you wittingly or unwittingly applied a form of intergenerational fairness and a long-term perspective. The fourth is that you explicitly understand you are not separate to the context – your experiences and outcomes are dependent on your surroundings and the behaviors of others.

This thought experiment brings forward an understanding of the need to find strategies and modes of operating that are good for the individual, good for others and good for the collective operating context (our surroundings). Further, the possibilities for those that come after us are bound to the choices of today and thus the challenge is to enhance, or at the very least preserve, their opportunities. This thinking is the foundation of the Future Normal approach – helping businesses operate meaningfully in our surroundings and purposefully to benefit itself and society.

A TIMELINE

Turning to the second aspect of Figure 2.1, the timeline and key moments in the development of business thinking. The timeline starts with the human/nature split that informed Western thought during the Age of Enlightenment.[9] This conceptual model that humans are separate to all that surrounds them – nature – is often described as the Cartesian dualism. This is in reference to the philosopher René Descartes and his mind/matter split, which treats humans and our surroundings as separate categories, a peculiarity of Western thought and not something that is part of the worldview of Indigenous cultures.[10] This peculiarity of Western thought is quite obviously a fallacy, as we are physically made of the Earth, not separate from it. The challenge of this split is that it shows itself in the core of business theory.[11] The convention of business theory is to treat our surroundings – our oceans, rivers, forests, air, the place where we all live and thus our societies – as being little more than a repository of opportunities and threats that the business should exploit.[12] As such, all that is 'outside' the business is dehumanized and considered as something that threatens its success.

During the late 1800s and early 1900s, business schools began to be established and a desire to have business theory treated as a 'hard' science emerged. That is, business schools were established to enable the profes-sionalism of corporate administrators, a cadre of individuals who wielded power but at the time lacked the enhanced social status of doctors and members of the clergy, who studied a codified and consolidated body of knowledge at a higher education institute. Consequently, with the estab-lishment of business schools, the question arose as to what foundation the theory of business should be built upon. At the time, social sciences such as business studies suffered in relative standing as they necessarily dealt in subjective issues, because business is embedded in human society and thus social sciences were considered not hard or 'rational' enough.[13] To counter this critique, business theory built itself around a central stem of numerical economics for two key reasons. First, economics had intellec-tual weight via the works of Adam Smith and his contemporaries a cen-tury or more before.[14] Second, economics was in the process of turning towards a 'hard' quantitative edge, particularly as prescribed by Lionel Robbins in his 1932 An Essay on the Nature and Significance of Economic Science,[15] leading to the neoclassical idea of profit maximization as the sole pur-pose of business[16]. From this numerical economic central stem, business theory has developed, and in so doing business theory has been reduced to numbers – dehumanized. This dehumanization has then logically been applied to everything else – our surroundings, our society and even to employees. For example, one of the early pioneers of modern business theory was American mechanical engineer Frederick Taylor, whose the-ories of scientific management took a perspective that considered human laborers as little more than automatons.[17] Of course, this is not the world anyone of us lives in, our organizations are collectives of people who are both emotional and rational.

Moving to the 1920s, a study conducted by the USA's National Bureau of Economic Research concluded that the desire to consume, and therefore the need to produce, had no limits. This is because human wants are never satisfied, as when one want is satisfied it will make way for a new want, endlessly.[18] Consequently, the view that economic growth is unfettered emerged. It remains the dominant position of most macroeconomic theory and is engrained in the rhetoric of politicians and central bankers the world over. In the 1930s the first set of comprehensive national accounts was developed in the USA. This set of accounts captured the monetary value of transactions in an economy. The key metric to arise from the national accounts is Gross Domestic Product (GDP).[19] Despite significant criticism,[20] this number has become a proxy measure of progress and the welfare of a society. Thus, human wellbeing and, in turn, the businesses that underpin economies are reducible to numbers and again dehumanized.

Moving through to the post-Second World War period and the Cold War, the dichotomy was between the American way versus the Soviet way, capitalism and markets vs. communism and central planning. As history shows, capitalism and markets prevailed, enshrining the importance of an individual firm pursuing its profits and reinforcing a view that individual and collective welfare is optimized through organizations engaged in competition. This perspective was supercharged by Milton Friedman, a Professor of Economics at the University of Chicago who, in the 1960s and '70s, advanced the idea of shareholder primacy,[21] arguing that the only responsibility of managers was to make profits for owners while broader concerns, such as societal development and environmental conditions, should be left to government.[22] These ideas were reinforced in the 1980s by the politics of Margaret Thatcher in the UK and Ronald Reagan in the USA, and because this was a politics in which social and economic outcomes were considered a result of individual choice not societal structures, established norms that businesses should be concerned about their workers and their lives were eroded.[23]

In a bid to counter the narrative of shareholder primacy, in 1984 philosopher and Professor of Business Administration R. Edward Freeman published *Strategic Management: A Stakeholder Approach*, widening the aperture on who and what matters in business.[24] Nevertheless, shareholder primacy continued to prosper, and the key duty of managers remained profit maximisation, seeking the highest revenue delivered at the lowest possible cost. By way of an aside, it should be noted that the ability to profit maximize is a myth, a theoretical construct, as to truly maximize profit a business leader would need to know all possibilities and outcomes – which, obviously, is impossible. Hence in actuality profit has always been, at best, optimized within a given context of what is knowable.

During the 1980s, Michael Porter, a Harvard Professor considered a founder of modern corporate strategy, staked his claim within business theory. His books on competitive strategy and competitive advantage reinforced that at the core of business theory the only concern is the advantage one firm has over another, and that advantage shows itself as the ability to earn higher returns. Further, in this pursuit of higher returns, a business is subject to competitive forces from all sides that are trying to prevent it succeeding. Porter's five forces, as they are now commonly known, are the threat of new entrants, the bargaining power of customers, the bargaining power of suppliers, the intense rivalry of competitors, and the threat of substitute services or products.[25] Consequently, the ambition of the business – and by default its leaders – should be to control those forces. It should be noted that these forces are us, we humans, as buyers (customers), suppliers, employees, innovators – and thus the control is of us. To close the 1980s and almost as a crowning edifice of this thinking, albeit not the end of it, 1987 saw the release of the Oliver Stone directed film *Wall Street*. In this film, one of the central characters, Gordon Gekko, played by Michael Douglas, utters the phrase "Greed, for lack of a better word, is good. Greed is right. Greed works."[26]

This line from *Wall Street* – and more widely what suffuses the thinking in business theory – is the idea that both individual and collective welfare are maximized through the pursuit of individual self-interest, an idea often attributed to Adam Smith and his 1776 work *An Inquiry into the Nature and Causes of the Wealth of Nations*.[27] That greed and individual profit 'maximization' is best for all, when greed itself is defined by an individual pursuing gains at the expense of others, is obviously a fallacy.

Nevertheless, despite its fallacies, these perspectives prevail, with much business education and received 'wisdom' in the business community promoting the notion that it is right for business leaders to operate as if they are eternally ravenous profit hunters operating in a dehumanized jungle, where they are in a fight for their survival through seeking opportunities for profit while at the same time avoiding threats (costs). This is a fantasy. Businesses are of us and part of us, that dehumanized jungle is where we all live, those profit opportunities are paid for by us, those threats are borne by us. Businesses do not operate in a dehumanized world; they shape us, and we shape them. As a separate thought experiment, consider how many of your wants in life were put into your mind by businesses. It will be more than you are comfortable with.

While the fallacies prevailed, they were not unchallenged. For example, Rachel Carson's Silent Spring, published in 1962, and the Earthrise picture of 1968[28] highlighted the fallacy that humans and nature, and in turn businesses and their surroundings, are separate. Carson's book outlined the challenges of the indiscriminate use of pesticides and their impact on birds and wildlife, and thus the desired state of our surroundings (we tend to like to hear birds singing). The Earthrise image highlights how our planet is an oasis of life in space and that there are no actual hard borders separating anything, our Earth is one interconnected system. The additional power of the Earthrise image is that it reinforces that all humans have been, currently are and will be for the foreseeable future, sourced from and existing on planet Earth. It's an image that reminds and reinforces that any one of us is Earth stuff and that the clothes we are wearing, have worn or thrown away, the food we are eating, have eaten or desire, all our material items, are all Earth stuff. In short, the Earth is a total service provider.

The implications of these understandings are brought to the fore in Barry Commoner's 1971 book The Closing Circle: Nature, Man, and Technology.[29] In its opening chapter, Commoner shapes what he considers evident generalizations into the following four laws of ecology: (1) Everything is connected to everything else, we live in a single connected system with no borders; (2) Everything must go somewhere, there is no 'away'; (3) Nature knows best, any major human-initiated change in a natural system is likely to be detrimental to that system; and (4) There is no such thing as a free lunch, every gain is won at some cost. Thus, what we do impacts the system and adjusts its balance, the rearrangement of our surroundings costs other parts of it. Further, we do not throw things away as there is no 'away' on our materially closed planet, rather we put our solid waste out of sight and we dilute our gaseous and liquid wastes by emitting them into the air we breathe, or into our oceans and waterways.

The lack of separation between humans and their surroundings and that there is no 'away' is reinforced by Kenneth Boulding in his influential 1966 essay 'The Economics of the Coming Spaceship Earth'.[30]

Boulding argues that we need to move the metaphor of actors within our economy from the cowboy to the spaceman. The cowboy always has a new frontier to move on to, to exploit and pollute, and thus the cowboy can pursue unbounded growth. However, our Earth has limits and is more akin to a spaceship, so it requires us to consider our development, the impact of pollutants and the ongoing viability of the life-support systems that sustain us.

> I am tempted to call the open economy the "cowboy economy," the cowboy being symbolic of the illimitable plains and also associated with reckless, exploitative, romantic, and violent behavior, which is characteristic of open societies. The closed economy of the future might similarly be called the "spaceman" economy, in which the Earth has become a single spaceship, without unlimited reservoirs of anything, either for extraction or for pollution, and in which, therefore, man must find his place in a cyclical ecological system...(pp. 7–8)

In the same year that the film *Wall Street* was released, how we live on our planet entered mainstream consciousness via the United Nations publication *Our Common Future*. This publication is a grand narrative that argues our purpose is to develop in a manner that does not compromise those who come after us. This was followed in 2012 with the publication of *Resilient People, Resilient Planet: A Future Worth Choosing*, a twenty-five-year update to *Our Common Future*. In a clear shift in emphasis from the earlier publication, which places the onus for action on government, *Resilient People, Resilient Planet* argues that corporate strategists are the key to future prosperity, acknowledging that we live in a world where businesses are the primary tools through which our interests are realized. Placing the responsibility for our future prosperity on business and the corporate world demands a different view of business than that in conventional business theory.

During this period counter narratives about how we should measure progress at a societal level also began to gain momentum. In 1990 the United Nations published the Human Development Index, devised by late economist Mahbub ul Haq to emphasize that people and their capabilities should be the ultimate criteria for assessing the development of a country, not economic growth alone. The index consists of three dimensions and four indicators: Health (life expectancy at birth), education (mean and expected years of schooling) and living stands (per capita gross national income). The Index has since been augmented to include adjustments for inequality, gender, gender inequality and planetary pressures.[31] In 2011 the Organization for Economic Coordination and Development (OECD) launched its Better Life Index. This Index consists of 11 measures ranging from civic engagement to work-life balance, and encourages users to choose their own relative weightings for each measure, which can have a significant impact on a nation's ranking.[32]

To bring us up to date, a shift towards an understanding that business is about more than money, and that businesses are key shapers of our societies and surroundings is now being reinforced by key business leaders. For example, in 2018 Larry Fink, the Chairman and CEO of BlackRock, the world's largest asset manager with approximately US$10 trillion in assets under management, wrote an open letter to CEOs stating that companies will not realize their full potential if they do not positively contribute to society.[33] Further, in 2019 the Business Roundtable of America adopted a new statement on the purpose of a corporation that challenges shareholder primacy and argues the purpose of a corporation is to deliver value for all stakeholders,[34] and a year later the Davos Manifesto argued businesses should engage with all stakeholders to create value.[35]

To summarize, there is a shift, and although there is still much to change, because history haunts, the new is starting to emerge and is gathering momentum, moving from the fringe to the mainstream. A new that recognizes a fundamental truth – businesses are not separate to us.

MOVING FORWARD – DON'T BE HAUNTED

The journey of this chapter has been to reflect on resistance to change, a thought experiment and some history of business thinking. It has highlighted how resistance to change can be embedded in our sense of self, yet businesses continually desire new thinking. The thought experiment reinforced how our context has changed and that the logical implication of this is to adjust strategies. The timeline highlighted some of the key waypoints in the development of business theory, noting that this timeline does not capture every aspect. In so doing, the aim of this chapter has been to show how there can be, in the case of business theory, a mismatch between our mental models and our lived reality. This mismatch is always the case with theories, they are always an approximation. However, the dehumanization of business theory has been particularly egregious given it is so obviously a fallacy and that businesses shape so much of our world. As you read this, virtually all that you are wearing, looking at and have eaten or drunk today has been brought to you by business and it is all Earth stuff. This is our physical grounding no matter which conceptual models we choose to apply. It may have been okay to operate with faulty logic when there were fewer of us on the planet, but not anymore. The costs are coming forward, perhaps most clearly seen in our changing climate.

This history of thinking in categories – humans here, other (separate) things over there – has run out of time. The realities of the Earthrise picture, Barry Commoner's four laws and the need to conceptualize our economy as operating on a spaceship rather than an endless frontier are coming to the fore. Likewise, thinking that the pursuit of individual wealth without consideration of the impacts on others somehow leads to the best outcomes for all is fraying at the edges, if it ever made sense. The costs are no longer out of sight. Our world is plagued with crises, including climate change, biodiversity loss, inequality, access to healthcare, ocean acidification and forest loss to name only those that spring immediately to mind.

Our society and our surroundings, the place where we live, what is around us, these are being eroded as we rearrange our material world in the pursuit of business success. Yet they are the foundations of business success; business does not float free. We treat our society and surroundings as if they are the tools of business, things to be continually controlled and manipulated to enable business profits. This is backward thinking; businesses are our tools for our ends. Businesses are formed by and of people, they are the tools we can and must use to enable all of us to thrive.

Moving forward, business leaders are evermore seen as the enablers of thriving societies and surroundings.[36] However, to shift these responsibilities to businesses is not without its difficulties. Business leaders are not elected by wider society and the history of the past still haunts, not least because convention, pursuing profit as if the world outside the interests of shareholders does not matter is simpler. However, the simple and naive notion of numbers alone is over; businesses need to operate in our world as it is and always has been. To do this they need to rehumanize and ask new questions, questions such as "Does our strategy enable a world we or our children would want to live in?" This type

Old Understanding – 2D	New Understanding - 3D
Humans and Nature are Separate	Humans & Nature never Separate
c2bn people	c8bn people
Profit Maximization	Profit Optimization
Cowboy Economy	Spaceship Economy
Categorical Thinking	Integrated Thinking
Business Individualism	Business shapes our Society and Surroundings
332ppm in 1975	414ppm in 2021

Figure 2.2 The shift required

of question drives the shift in thinking that is required and is captured schematically in Figure 2.2.

Figure 2.2 aims to highlight how to shift from considering business as something that is only about money and that exists in a blank exploitable space to understanding that business exists within an economy that is of our society and our surroundings, and these all interact to impact our ability to thrive. By making this shift, business' long-term value will be realized. This new understanding of business is what frames our future, the topic of the next chapter.

NOTES

1 For example, in 2017 Harvard University researchers Geoffrey Supran and Naomi Oreskes published a series of works clearly outlining climate-science denial by ExxonMobil. An interview with Geoffrey Supran published in The Harvard Gazette can be found here: https://news.harvard.edu/gazette/story/2021/09/oil-compan ies-discourage-climate-action-study-says/.

2 In 1824 French mathematician and physicist Joseph Fourier published an article hypothesizing that gases in the atmosphere acted to trap heat from the Sun. In 1856 Eunice Newton Foote published a paper reporting on an experiment that tested the heat-trapping abilities of different gases, including carbon dioxide, an experiment that was repeated in 1859 by John Tyndall (after whom the United Kingdom's Tyndall Centre for Climate Change Research is named). In 1896, Swedish physicist Svante Arrhenius created the world's first model of climate change, predicting that a doubling of the amount of carbon dioxide in the atmosphere would add 41 to 43 degrees Fahrenheit (5 to 6 degrees Celsius) to the Earth's temperature; a result that is remarkably consistent with the estimates of modern climate models. See a more detailed discussion here: https://daily.jstor.org/how-19th-century-scientists-predicted-glo bal-warming/.

3 Climate Watch, an online platform managed by the World Resources Institute, provides detailed data on greenhouse gas emissions. See: https://www.climatewatchdata.org/.

4 Brandpie, a global purpose-driven transformation consultancy produces an annual CEO Purpose Report that documents the findings of a survey of CEOs from around the globe. We collaborated with Brandpie on their 2022 report, adding a question on the degree of overlap between the CEO's personal purpose and that of their organization. The mean response, on a scale of 1 (no overlap) to 5 (total overlap) was 4.0, with 40% of respondents selecting '5'. All Brandpie CEO Purpose Reports can be found here: https://www.brandpie.com/thinking/ceo-purpose-report.

5 As estimated by the United Nations World Population Prospects 2022. The summary of results can be found here: https://www.un.org/development/desa/pd/sites/www.un.org.development.desa.pd/files/wpp2022_summary_of_results.pdf.

6 This takes us (very briefly) to thermodynamics, the science of energy. Energy is the potential to do work or supply heat. Work is involved when matter is changed in structure, in physical or chemical nature, or in location. In an open system, both energy and matter can be exchanged with its environment. An individual organism, for example a human being, is an open system. In a closed system, such as the Earth, energy but not matter can be exchanged. The Earth's sources of external energy is the Sun.

7 Discussed later in this chapter, the second law of ecology proposed by Barry Commoner is *Everything must go somewhere*, there is no 'waste' in nature and there is no 'away', matter can only be transferred from place to place or converted from one molecular form to another. This can be linked to the materials balance principle in economics, which states that economic activity does not, in a material sense, create anything, rather it simply transforms material so that it is more valuable to humans. This also implies that all material extracted from the Earth into the economic system must at some point be returned to the Earth, albeit in a transformed state.

8 John Rawls was a 21st century philosopher who sought to establish the principles of a just society. To do this Rawls employs the device of imagining a hypothetical state, the 'original position', prior to any agreement about principles of justice, the organization of social institutions and the distribution of material rewards or endowments. In this original position, individuals exist behind a 'veil of ignorance', where, for example, they are unaware of their gender, ethnicity or social status. Rawls concludes that under these circumstances, people would unanimously agree on the following fundamental principles of justice. First, the liberty principle, which establishes equal basic liberties for all. Second, the equality principle, which states that social and economic inequalities must satisfy the following conditions: a) they are attached to offices and positions that are open to all (equality of opportunity) and b) they are arranged in such a way as to be of the greatest benefit to the least-advantaged members of society (referred to as Rawls' difference principle).

9 Preceded by the Scientific Revolution, the Enlightenment was a period of rigorous scientific, political, and philosophical discourse that took place in Europe from the late 17th to early 19th century.

10 Aboriginal scholar Tyson Yunkaporta's 2019 book *Sand Talk: How Indigenous Thinking Can Save the World* provides valuable insight into connections between Indigenous philosophies and sustainable development.

11 In their 1995 article in the *Academy of Management Review*, Thomas Gladwin, James Kennelly and Tara-Shelomith Krause note that modern management theory is constricted by a fractured epistemology, which both separates humanity from nature and truth from morality. The authors argue that reintegration is necessary if organizational science is to support ecologically and socially sustainable development, concluding that transforming management theory and practice so that they positively contribute to sustainable development is the greatest challenge facing the Academy. See: Gladwin, T., Kennelly, J. & Krause, T-S. (1995). Shifting paradigms for sustainable development: Implications for management theory and research. *Academy of Management Review*, 20(4), 874-907. https://doi.org/10.5465/amr.1995.9512280024.

12 In 2016 Nick published an article that reviewed the conceptualization of the environment within best-selling strategy textbooks in the United Kingdom and Australia. In the article it was argued that strategists are key actors in the realization of sustainable outcomes, and that the constructs those individuals learn from texts are potentially key to the realization of sustainable outcomes. The review revealed that constructs in the textbooks offer a sclerotic, dehumanized view of the environment that is partitioned into external and internal categories by an organizational boundary, a limitation that will not foster sustainable outcomes. See: Barter, N. (2016). Strategy textbooks and the environment construct: Are the texts enabling strategists to realize sustainable outcomes? *Organization & Environment*, 29(3), 332-366. https://doi.org/10.1177/108602661 6638130.

13 For further discussion on the history of business schools see: Khurana, R. (2007). *From Higher Aims to Hired Hands. The Social Transformation of American Business Schools and the Unfulfilled Promise of Management*. Princeton University Press.

14 Political economy as it was known emerged as a distinct field of study in the mid-18th century, with notable figures including Adam Smith (1723–90), François Quesnay (1694–1774), David Ricardo (1772–1823), Thomas Malthus (1766-1834) and John Stuart Mill (1806–1873).

15 Robbins, L. (1932). *An Essay on the Nature and Significance of Economic Science*, London: Macmillan.

16 It should be noted that this reduction of the purpose of business to a single objective was simply for mathematical convenience; single-objective optimization is much easier to solve than multiple-objective optimization.

17 Taylor first put forward these theories in his 1911 monograph *The Principles of Scientific Management* and Taylorism as it is now known can still be seen throughout modern management theory.

18 As stated in the report "…wants are almost insatiable; that one want satisfied makes way for another. The conclusion is that economically we have a boundless field before us; that there are new wants which will make way endlessly for newer wants, as fast as they are satisfied". National Bureau of Economic Research and Hoover, H. (1929). *Report of the Committee on Recent Economic Changes of the President's Conference on Unemployment*. Available here: http://www.nber.org/chapters/c4950.

19 Gross Domestic Product (GDP) and Gross National Product (GNP) are terms often treated synonymously, although there is a difference. The former measures the value

of economic activity that takes place within a nation's borders, the latter measures the value of economic activity by a nation's permanent residents or citizens, no matter where that activity takes place.

20 There are many problems with using GDP/GNP as a measure of economic welfare. The principal difficulty is that non-market transactions are not recorded. Thus, GDP/GNP ignores the cost of environmental damage, the value of housework or childcare and voluntary work, among many other activities that have real impacts (positive and negative) on our wellbeing. This has to led to critiques from several commentators, but perhaps none as colorful as this quote from ecological economist Herman Daly, who in his 1973 book *Toward a Steady-State Economy* wrote "We take the real costs of increasing GNP as measured by the defensive expenditures incurred to protect ourselves from the unwanted side effects of production, and add these expenditures to GNP rather than subtract them. We count the real costs as benefits - this is hyper-growth mania. Since the net benefit of growth can never be negative with this Alice-in-Wonderland accounting system, the rule becomes 'grow forever' or at least until it kills you - and then count your funeral expenses as further growth". (p.40).

21 An idea advanced by Friedman in his 1962 book *Capitalism and Freedom*, shareholder primacy is a theory in corporate governance holding that shareholder interests should be assigned priority relative to all other stakeholders.

22 These views are clearly expounded in an opinion piece Friedman wrote for the New York Times in 1970. A digitized copy from the New York Times archive can be found here: https://www.nytimes.com/1970/09/13/archives/a-friedman-doctrine-the-social-responsibility-of-business-is-to.html.

23 For further discussion on the emergence of neoliberalism under Thatcher and Regan, and those that followed see: Steger, M. & Roy, R. (2021). *Neoliberalism: A Very Short Introduction* (2nd edition), Oxford University Press.

24 We will return to Freeman and stakeholder theory in Chapter 6.

25 Although by no means his only contribution to the field, Porter is perhaps best known for this five forces framework, which he first described in a 1979 Harvard Business Review article 'How Competitive Forces Shape Strategy'.

26 Critically acclaimed and a box office success, the film has come to be seen as the archetypal portrayal of 1980s excess. For further analysis of the film see: https://www.dressedcinema.com/blog/2011/05/analyzed-wall-street.

27 Smith's support for unbridled capitalism and his belief in the welfare maximizing outcomes from free markets is almost certainly overstated. Smith in fact only mentions an invisible hand once in *The Wealth of Nations*, in a paragraph discussing the social benefits derived from the free movement of capital. A critique of Smith's beliefs and the modern interpretation of those is provided by Political scientist Paul Sagar and can be found here: https://aeon.co/essays/we-should-look-closely-at-what-adam-smith-actually-believed.

28 Taken by astronaut Bill Anders on Christmas Eve 1968 as the Apollo 8 spacecraft rounded the dark side of the moon, the Earthrise picture has been variously described as the most influential environmental photo ever taken and the beginning of the environmental movement. See: https://en.wikipedia.org/wiki/Earthrise.

29 Commoner, B. (1971) *The Closing Circle: Nature, Man, and Technology* (1st edition), Alfred A. Knopf. Subsequently reprinted in 1972 with the more explicit title *The Closing Circle: Confronting the Environmental Crisis.*

30 Boulding, K. (1966). The economics of the coming spaceship earth. In Jarrett, H. (ed.) *Environmental Quality in a Growing Economy*, Resources for the Future and Johns Hopkins University Press, pp. 3-14.

31 We will return to discuss measures of progress in Chapter 7. Further information about the United Nations' Human Development Reports and the Human Development Index can be found here: https://hdr.undp.org/.

32 For example, if all measures are weighted equally, Norway is ranked first. However, if education is more heavily weighted, Norway slips to fourth and Finland moves from fifth to first. See: https://www.oecdbetterlifeindex.org/#/11111111111.

33 See: https://www.blackrock.com/corporate/investor-relations/2018-larry-fink-ceo-letter.

34 Since 1978 the Business Roundtable has periodically issued statements on the principles of corporate governance. Between 1997 and 2019 all statements endorsed the principle of shareholder primacy. In a significant shift, the 2019 statement outlined what the Roundtable considered to be a modern standard for corporate responsibility, committing to deliver value to customers, invest in employees, deal fairly and ethically with suppliers, support the communities in which they work and generate long-term value for shareholders. See: https://www.businessroundtable.org/purposeanniversary.

35 Davos is the name given to the annual meeting of the World Economic Forum, after the Swiss town in which it is held. The 2020 Manifesto opens with the following statement: "The purpose of a company is to engage all its stakeholders in shared and sustained value creation. In creating such value, a company serves not only its shareholders, but all its stakeholders – employees, customers, suppliers, local communities and society at large. The best way to understand and harmonize the divergent interests of all stakeholders is through a shared commitment to policies and decisions that strengthen the long-term prosperity of a company". See: https://www.weforum.org/agenda/2019/12/davos-manifesto-2020-the-universal-purpose-of-a-company-in-the-fourth-industrial-revolution/.

36 This is particularly true in the context of tackling climate change. See for example this 2022 opinion piece by Time Magazine correspondent Justin Worland: https://time.com/6166178/earths-future-big-business/.

Three

As the saying goes, prediction is difficult, especially about the future.[1] Yet prediction is core to business strategy – one never writes strategies about the past, always about times to come. Hence, every strategist knows they will need to construct a narrative about their business and its future prosperity. To develop the narrative, the strategist relies on the business' purpose, vision and values, and, most importantly, the expectations of stakeholders. These expectations oscillate around views on, for example, whether the business sells a little or a lot, what levels of investment are required, what competencies and capabilities need developing, which suppliers need to be engaged, what materials will be used and how goods or services will be distributed. Distilling these expectations is critical to strategy development, so negotiating and navigating these expectations is a key skill. Once distilled, the strategy will be presented back to stakeholders to develop further iterations. Ultimately the final strategy will emerge, with a narrative typically following a form that is akin to the Hero's Journey.[2] That is, the narrative will cover the challenge or challenges the business is facing; a rationale for why the old strategy is out of date; a restatement of the purpose, vision and values of the business; and how, within these parameters, there is a clarion call for the business to overcome the challenge in the manner being prescribed. From this basis, the means of vanquishing the challenge or challenges are outlined and the future success of this course of action cemented through predictions of key indicators such as market size, market share, revenues and returns. Invariably, these predictions will follow a pattern where the agreed measures of success (typically revenue or profit) uptick in three to five years' time. On the understanding that these are accurate,

DOI: 10.4324/9781003360636-4

the strategy will be accepted and implemented before the process is repeated a few years later to address a new set of challenges.

To summarize, the strategy is pulled together through a process of iteration with stakeholders and is composed of a mix of narrative prose and numerical prediction. This is a process that almost all businesses follow, and it highlights how the 'truth' of any one strategy is rooted in belief. Embedded within this process are our worldviews. These are the logics that underpin how we believe the world works. Consequently, it is our worldview that informs our belief in a strategy and whether we think it makes sense. However, our worldviews are not fixed or monolithic, they continually evolve via an influx of information – albeit the haunting of history and our lack of mental flexibility can make us resistant to evolution and change.

As we turn to the coming decades, there are a plethora of predictions about what lies ahead (some of which are highlighted below). In highlighting predictions, we do not question the veracity of any specific one, because each has been formulated by experts via the scientific process. However, we do puncture the hope that lies in the shadow of billionaires' dreams of colonizing Mars, not from the perspective of whether it is technically feasible, but from the perspective of who is likely to be invited.

The aim of this chapter is to frame the future through reinforcing an aspect of business that is foundational and inarguable – namely, businesses are embedded in people and people are embedded in the planet. It is from this foundation that we frame what could be normal in the future, and the eight questions that are at the core of such a transformation.

PREDICTIONS AND FOUNDATIONS

Predictions about the coming decades include those related to environmental concerns such as climate change,[3][4] ocean acidification,[5] biodiversity decline and ecosystem collapse,[6] and those related to social and economic concerns, such as an increasing[7] and aging population,[8] the erosion of social cohesion,[9] the challenges of increased digitization, and geopolitical instability.[10] As we frame the future, there are significant challenges ahead, challenges that are creating evermore anxiety in the next generation[11].

Ground zero for all these predictions is our single planet, our pale blue dot.[12] This is the foundation that business leaders need to embrace;

everything needs to be navigated on a planet where there is no away, everything connects and there is no free lunch. This is ground zero.

This book and the Future Normal approach is about the inescapable; strategies are bound to being carried out on Earth. They are bound to being developed by humans, physical beings that are made of the Earth. This is and will always be the case, at least for the far foreseeable future. No matter the dreams of billionaires with their desire to colonize Mars, this colonization will not be for all of us, the eight billion of us currently on this planet. This is because first, Mars is much less hospitable than the top of Mount Everest[13] and to make it hospitable at a planetary scale is a project that we are yet to embark on. Second, it is unlikely everyone will be invited, even if it was technically feasible to move eight billion people to another planet. One estimate suggests that it could take as few as 110 people to successfully colonize Mars.[14] Hence, colonization is not likely to include a ticket for you, your children or even your children's children. The overwhelming majority of us are destined to continue living our lives and realizing our wellbeing on Earth for centuries, if not millennia, to come. Thus, while such dreams can matter in terms of helping propel our human story forward, this dream is not a practical solution: there is no Planet B.

Stepping back, our challenge is how we shape society and our surroundings. Innovation in this vein is necessary, as no matter what the future holds, we are going to be physical beings that breathe, eat, sleep and live in societies on Earth. Our wellbeing is reliant on the wellbeing of our society and Earth's ecosystems. Further, no matter how technology shifts the patterns of work, businesses will always be anthropologically rooted, they will always be of people. We often talk about businesses conceptually as if they were, for example, a machine or an organism. While such metaphors can be useful, they deny a fundamental truth: Businesses, like all organizations, are a coming together of people who co-ordinate their actions through their conversations about some shared idea of the future and what the business is attempting to achieve. Consequently, organizations and businesses are tools that are a means to an end and their acts are rooted in human-to-human conversations. Those conversations are informed by worldviews and all the information we exchange with others, be they human or non-human. This information might be messages from the media, messages from family, friends or neighbors, noticing a lack of birds in the sky or changing weather patterns, or the sight and smell of pollution in our local waterways and forests. We are receiving information through all our senses all the time.

Hence, even though the hierarchical organizing structure of businesses denotes power imbalances and a lack of egalitarian conversations, over the long-term, because our businesses are rooted in humans, there is little point to any strategy if it is not trying to enable us to thrive. This is very easy to say, and its logic is clear: We share one Earth. Yet this statement of the obvious is not how we behave. There are too many examples of businesses engaged in the pursuit of short-term returns at the expense of so much else, for example those involved in the production and sale of opioids, guns, sugary drinks, tobacco, fossil fuels ... the list goes on, all pursued while trying to lower wages bills and avoid taxes.[15]

We are not so naive as to believe that the era of pursuing returns at the expense of all else is over. However, such a pursuit is always short-term because, while perceptions can be manipulated, the laws of physics are immutable. Thus, no matter how hard strategists try, the mirage that businesses exist in dehumanized surroundings and that actions do not have an impact, or that the impact can be ignored, will eventually disappear. Hence, there may be a desire to delay the inevitable, but the fact that businesses exist in a world with no borders and that our strategies and the questions we ask of our businesses need to adapt, will ultimately prevail.

The previous chapter explained the shift in terms of business theory, but another way in which to explain the shift is to apply a simple test. This test is one we use with executives and MBA students alike. It consists of asking three questions: (1) Where is the environment? (2) Where is society? (3) Where is the economy? After a moment of reflection and invariably some doubt, as individuals are not sure if the questions contain a trick, these annoyingly simple questions have answers that are obvious. The environment, society and economy are everywhere.

Thus, respondents quickly realize that we and our businesses are caught up in a borderless imbroglio of economy, society and environment, the basis of which is our physicality. Our businesses are bound to our biology first. This realization, which is clear and obvious when we step back, is not the stuff of convention, yet it is the stuff of how we live and, in our view, this is the 'correct' starting point from which to develop strategies. It is the starting point that should become normal in the future.

This shift is happening. Climate change is an obvious example, it is forcing the issue as we are being backed into the management of our atmosphere through the control of greenhouse gas emissions. By extension, as we consider the predictions touched upon earlier, it is likely we are going to be forced into more and more management of the systems that surround us and we are part of. Systems that we previously took for granted. Managing these systems is, from an operational-efficiency perspective, a mistake, as few would recommend taking on that which we could avoid. However, in these challenges lies innovation, which will yield new opportunities. Further, and to close the circle on the dreams of billionaires, it makes little sense to colonize other planets unless we know how to ensure our thriving on this one. Caution is warranted as we attempt to solve these challenges, as our history of intervention in natural systems is not glorious, be it our overuse of pesticides killing bees and resulting in us needing to pollinate trees by hand or our destruction of mangrove forests increasing our susceptibility to storms, tsunamis and rising sea levels.[16]

FRAMING FOR FUTURE NORMAL STRATEGIES

So far, this chapter has outlined how business strategies are developed, sketched some predictions for the coming decades and reinforced the idea that no matter what, our businesses are of us. This, in our view, is the starting point from which to develop business strategy that should be normal in the future. This is not just because we say so, rather it is our materiality, the science of our situation, and is non-negotiable. We can negotiate different pay levels in an organization, different growth projections in a strategy, but we cannot negotiate away the fact that we are eating, breathing Earth-beings who live in societies and physical surroundings.

Building on this raises the question of what is a human? This is a question that can be explored philosophically. Our view is that we are Earth processes involved in the transformation of their surroundings and themselves. In practice this means that we consider humans as a conflation of their individuality, their community and their subjective and objective identity. The basis of this is outlined in Figure 3.1.[17]

As illustrated in Figure 3.1, our view is that humans and human well-being are developed across four zones: (1) Inside ourselves, in essence the stories we tell ourselves; (2) Objective measures outside of us such as our income and physical health; (3) Us with others, our relationships with others, our love of a place (topophilia) or loss of a place (solastalgia); and (4) The interactions between us and wider systems. The framework

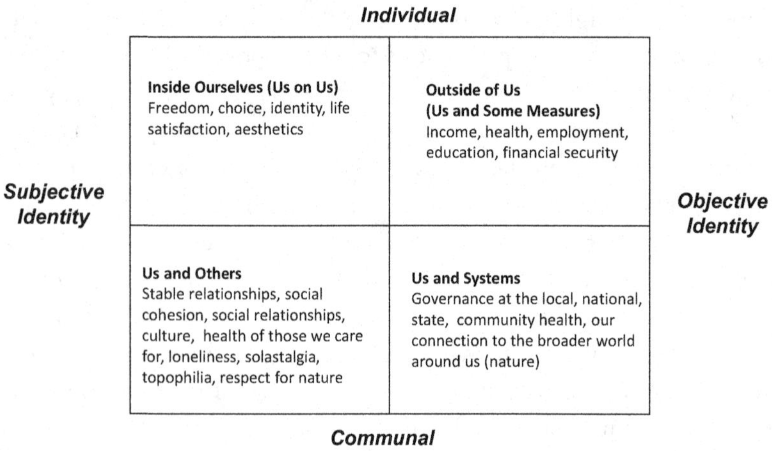

Inside Ourselves (Us on Us) Freedom, choice, identity, life satisfaction, aesthetics	Outside of Us (Us and Some Measures) Income, health, employment, education, financial security
Us and Others Stable relationships, social cohesion, social relationships, culture, health of those we care for, loneliness, solastalgia, topophilia, respect for nature	Us and Systems Governance at the local, national, state, community health, our connection to the broader world around us (nature)

Subjective Identity (left)   *Objective Identity* (right)

Communal

Figure 3.1 A model of being human/wellbeing

Figure adapted from Painter-Morland, M., Demuijnck, G. and Ornati, S., 2017. Sustainable development and well-being: A philosophical challenge. *Journal of Business Ethics*, 146(2), pp.295-311. https://doi.org/10.1007/s10551-017-3658-4.

depicted in this figure re-situates humans into a network of relationships rather than considering humans in a way that is removed from their contexts. To aid in this understanding it can be useful to consider the ends-means spectrum offered in Figure 3.2. This spectrum is a stylized version of that proposed by ecological economist Herman Daly[18] and adapted by systems thinker Donella Meadows among others.[19]

Placing businesses on this spectrum highlights how they tend to navigate the territory between intermediate means and intermediate ends, albeit many claim that their goods or services will provide happiness, harmony and transcendence. These claims notwithstanding, all rely on ultimate means – us and our surroundings – to operate. Building on this and referencing our earlier discussion of how businesses are tools whose acts are developed through conversations, five key aspects of businesses arise: (1) Businesses are not things, they are processes enabled through the acts of humans, they are the tools of humans; (2) The acts of businesses impact us, there are no separate spaces; (3) These acts of businesses result in responses that help shape us and our surroundings; (4) The acts of businesses are guided by the conversations we have and the questions we ask; and (5) The questions we ask are guided by our worldview, our

Ultimate Ends — **Wellbeing** - Happiness, Harmony, Identity, Self-realization, Transcendence

Theology & Ethics

Intermediate Ends — **Society and Rearranged Surroundings -** Health, wealth, leisure, mobility, knowledge, communication, consumer goods, education,..

Political Economy

Intermediate Means — **Businesses and Other Organizations -** Labour, tools, factories, processing,...

Science & Technology

Ultimate Means — **Earth (Us and Our Surroundings) -** Solar energy, biosphere, ecosystems, our materiality

Figure 3.2 Stylized ends-means spectrum

Figure adapted from Daly, H.E. and Farley, J., 2011. *Ecological Economics: Principles and Applications*. Island Press. 2nd edition, p.49 AND Daly, H.E. ed., 1980. *Economics, Ecology, Ethics: Essays Toward a Steady-state Economy*. San Francisco: W.H Freeman. p.9 AND Meadows, D.H., 1998. Indicators and information systems for sustainable development. p.42.

assumptions, and particularly our view of what we believe constitutes our wellbeing.

Consequently, to shift a business to act from an understanding that recognizes its embeddedness, it is necessary to shift the questions asked and potentially the worldview of the organizational participants. The eight questions at the core of this book are about enabling this shift. We recognize, however, that businesses will adopt this approach to varying degrees, or not at all. That is, businesses will operate on a scale ranging from those pursuing their outcomes with minimal regard for our surroundings and society to those that operate beyond the minimum and are attempting to lead. For simplicity, the ends of the scale we offer in Figure 3.3 are 'Bad Company' and 'Good Company'.

No matter what the future brings, it is likely that businesses will always exist across such a scale. Hence, the broader goal of embracing a Future Normal perspective is that the scale in Figure 3.3 shifts to the right and Bad Company in the future is closer to the position of Good

Framing the future

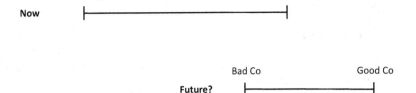

Figure 3.3 Bad company, good company scale

Company today, while Good Company of the future exists off the current scale, further to the right.

The eight questions we have put at the core of this book are an attempt to shift businesses and provide a way of enabling stakeholders to engage in conversations that open new challenges and opportunities, and ultimately develop new strategies. Questions that will in turn ensure the business operates with an understanding of its embeddedness while also shifting to the right on Figure 3.3. The subsequent chapters explain the questions more fully. However, by way of introduction, they are as follows:

1 Does your business' vision perpetuate a world you want to live in?
2 Is your business aligned with our world?
3 Does your business listen to all its stakeholders?
4 Does your business have the metrics?
5 Does your business use language that enables?
6 Does your business understand its footprint and tread carefully?
7 Does your business learn from nature?
8 Does your business lead by enabling others?

These eight questions provide an opportunity, if asked with curiosity, for business leaders to develop renewed strategies that will enable their businesses to act meaningfully and purposefully. In this regard, the questions are much more ambitious than those conventionally asked. This is because they don't take a money first perspective, rather they put us first. Thus, they view the business as a tool and push business leaders to consider more than simply making returns.

At one level the answer to any one of the eight questions can be yes, no or maybe. Such a closed response is fine, but the actual power of each question arises when the 'why' and 'what' of that closed response is explored. For example, why that answer? What does it imply?

Exploring the rationale for each question a little more, the first reinforces how businesses shape society, our surroundings and our lives. The second question explores the worldview of the individuals in the business and whether they understand their embeddedness or not, and if and how this may align across the business. As such, the question is exploring whether the business participants understand its ultimate means and, in turn, are they aligned to this. Taken together, these first two questions cover direction and culture, two aspects core to any strategy. From here, question three explores which stakeholders are listened to. The key to this is understanding that ensuring future prosperity brings forward new stakeholders, such as the next generation and non-humans. Question four explores how we measure success.

Turning to questions five through seven, these take a more internal perspective. Question five discusses the language of business, with a focus on two key facets: psychological distance and metaphors. The aim is to highlight the need to reduce psychological distance and use alternative metaphors. Question six discusses how hard the organization presses on our Earth, its footprint. Question seven explores operational processes and proffers that these could be improved by learning from nature. The final question, question eight, discusses how the business behaves relative to others. For example, whether the business is a catalyst for wider change or if it pursues old conventions of competitive advantage.

The next eight chapters explore each question in depth, presenting rationale, supporting theory and application. Each of these chapters will give you the confidence to shift your business towards a new approach, one that recognizes the fundamentals, one that is Future Normal.

A couple of things before you go further. There is no special reason for eight questions, it just happens that through application and work-shopping a total of eight emerged. Second, the questions are a starting point – you should feel free to adjust and develop them for your business. Third, don't expect transformation in a day, the questions provide permission to explore so that change will come.

NOTES

1 Although attributed to several people, including Mark Twain and New York Yankees player-come-manager Yogi Berra, this saying is most likely to have originated from Danish physicist Niels Bohr.

2 Popularized in Joseph Campbell's 1949 book *The Hero with a Thousand Faces*, the Hero's Journey or Monomyth is a narrative common across time and culture in which a heroic-protagonist sets out on journey, overcomes challenges or temptations, and then returns home transformed.

3 There is no shortage of scientific and popular literature outlining the potential impacts of climate change on humanity and our surroundings. The definitive source of scientific literature is the IPCC. The second part of the (most recent) Sixth Assessment Report is titled *Climate Change 2022: Impacts, Adaptation and Vulnerability*. In this, the IPCC observe that approximately 3.3 to 3.6 billion people live in contexts that are highly vulnerable to climate change and that global warming, reaching 1.5°C in the near-term, would cause unavoidable increases in multiple climate hazards and present multiple risks to ecosystems and humans. See: https://www.ipcc.ch/report/sixth-assessment-report-working-group-ii/.

4 For almost two decades the World Economic Forum has produced an annual Global Risks Report, drawing upon a survey of over 1000 experts across academia, business, government, the international community and civil society. Climate-related risks dominate the most recent (2023) report, taking the top five spots in the list of the ten most severe risks facing humanity over the next decade. The full report can be found here: https://www3.weforum.org/docs/WEF_Global_Risks_Report_2023.pdf.

5 See this educational resource on ocean acidification from the US Department of Commerce's National Oceanic and Atmospheric Administration: https://www.noaa.gov/education/resource-collections/ocean-coasts/ocean-acidification.

6 Swiss Re, a reinsurance company based in Zurich, produces a Biodiversity and Ecosystem Services Index to assess which economic sectors are most reliant on nature and evaluate the exposure of individual countries to declining biodiversity. The Index aggregates ten indicators of biodiversity and ecosystem services and provides those data at a 1km^2 resolution. A 2020 study based on the results of the Index suggested that a fifth of countries worldwide were at risk from ecosystem collapse as biodiversity declines. Further details about the Index can be found here: https://www.swissre.com/institute/research/topics-and-risk-dialogues/climate-and-natural-catastrophe-risk/expertise-publication-biodiversity-and-ecosystems-services.html#/. A press release discussing the 2020 study can be found here: https://www.swissre.com/media/press-release/nr-20200923-biodiversity-and-ecosystems-services.html.

7 The United Nations predict that the world's population will reach 8.5 billion in 2030 and increase further to 9.7 billion in 2050 and 10.4 billion by 2100. See: https://www.un.org/en/global-issues/population.

8 An opinion piece published by the International Monetary Fund and authored by researchers from Harvard University's T.H. Chan School of Public Health argues that the most formidable demographic challenge facing the world is no longer rapid population growth, but population aging. See: https://www.imf.org/en/Publications/fandd/issues/Series/Analytical-Series/aging-is-the-real-population-bomb-bloom-zucker.

9 Erosion of social cohesion and societal polarization was ranked seventh in the World Economic Forum's 2023 Global Risks Report list of the ten most severe risks facing humanity over the next decade.

10 Widespread cybercrime and cyber insecurity and geoeconomic confrontation were ranked eighth and ninth respectively in the World Economic Forum's 2023 Global Risks Report list of the ten most severe risks facing humanity over the next decade.

11 The rise of eco-anxiety in young people is well documented. For example, an article published in *The Lancet Planetary Health* reports the results of a survey of 10,000 children and young people (aged 16–25 years) in ten countries (Australia, Brazil, Finland, France, India, Nigeria, Philippines, Portugal, the UK, and the USA). Data were collected on participants' thoughts and feelings about climate change, and government responses to climate change. The findings of this survey are as follows: Respondents across all countries were worried about climate change (59% were very or extremely worried and 84% were at least moderately worried). More than 50% reported each of the following emotions: sad, anxious, angry, powerless, helpless and guilty. More than 45% of respondents said their feelings about climate change negatively affected their daily life and functioning, and many reported a high number of negative thoughts about climate change (e.g., 75% said that they think the future is frightening and 83% said that they think people have failed to take care of the planet). See: Hickman, C., Marks, E., Pihkala, P., Clayton, S., Lewandowski, R.E., Mayall, E.E., ... & van Susteren, L. (2021). Climate anxiety in children and young people and their beliefs about government responses to climate change: a global survey. *The Lancet Planetary Health*, 5(12), e863-e873. https://doi.org/10.1016/S2542-5196(21)00278-3.

12 The Pale Blue Dot is a photograph of Earth taken by the Voyager 1 space probe at the request of astronomer and author Carl Sagan, who coined the term and reflected upon the photo in his 1994 book *Pale Blue Dot: A Vision of the Human Future in Space*. This reflection has subsequently been recorded and is available on YouTube: https://www.youtube.com/watch?v=GO5FwsblpT8. Take the time to watch this clip. We frequently use this as a starting point for conversations with clients and students as it powerfully reinforces the bounds within which we all operate.

13 A point made by Amazon founder Jeff Bezos in reference to the purported plans of space exploration rival Elon Musk. See: https://www.businessinsider.com/jeff-bezos-mount-everest-challenge-mars-spacex-elon-musk-2019-3.

14 The minimum number of people required to colonize Mars was calculated by French Professor Jean-Marc Salotti and published in the journal *Scientific Reports*. The paper can be found here: https://www.nature.com/articles/s41598-020-66740-0.

15 American sociologist Gerald Davis provides a searing critique of corporate behaviour and the destructive incentives inherent in shareholder capitalism in the *Journal of Management Studies*. He argues that the surest path to getting corporations to 'behave themselves' is more democracy, greater worker control from below and more effective regulation from above. See: Davis, G. (2021). Corporate purpose needs democracy. *Journal of Management Studies*, 58(3), 902-913. https://doi.org/10.1111/joms.12659.

16 Phoebe Weston, biodiversity reporter for British newspaper *The Guardian*, outlines seven ways in which human intervention in the natural world has led to deadly

outcomes, including the loss of bees in China and mangroves in Indonesia, Sri Lanka, India and Thailand. See: https://www.theguardian.com/environment/2022/nov/22/what-happens-when-humans-meddle-with-nature-aoe.

17 This figure is adapted from: Painter-Morland, M., Demuijnck, G., & Ornati, S. (2017). Sustainable development and well-being: A philosophical challenge. *Journal of Business Ethics*, 146(2), 295-311. https://doi.org/10.1007/s10551-017-3658-4.

18 Herman Daly first proposed the ends-means spectrum in his 1973 book *Towards a Steady-State Economy*. A fierce critic of mainstream economics, Daly argued that economics was positioning itself too narrowly in the middle of the spectrum, treating economic growth as the ultimate end rather than as one means to an end.

19 See for example: Meadows, D. (1999), 'Indicators and information systems for sustainable development' in *The Earthscan Reader in Sustainable Cities* (pp. 364-393), Routledge, or Raworth, K. (2017). *Doughnut Economics: Seven Ways to Think Like a 21st-century Economist*, Chelsea Green Publishing.

THE CHALLENGE QUESTIONS
PART II

Four

The vision of a business can be considered its aspiration, the outcomes that it would like to realize. When setting the direction of a business, the question that is often *not* asked is the one that is the title of this chapter: Does your business' vision perpetuate a world you want to live in?

This question is often overlooked because conventional theories and mindsets typically concentrate on a vision that is about the business alone. Take the time now and ask yourself: Does your business have a vision that, if realized, would create a world in which you want to live? Does that vision result in a better society for you, your family, your children? Does that vision result in better surroundings for you and future generations? Or is the vision about the company alone, its glory, its performance?

Turning to specific elements of the vision, does society get a mention? Is the vision about some of us or all of us? If only some of us, why do some people count for more than others? Can you be sure your progeny will always be in the 'right' group? Is the vision generous or meagre? Who is getting great in the vision and why, to what end? And, finally, ask yourself: Could the vision of the business be changed to encompass greater outcomes for all?

Asking these questions cuts to the core of your business. They speak to its direction – the idealized future it wants to realize, what you and your colleagues are working towards – and it builds a bridge to the mindset of the employees.

A vision matters because it is part of the narrative framework of the business. The vision, along with the purpose, mission and values

Does your business' vision perpetuate a world you want to live in?

39

DOI: 10.4324/9781003360636-6

enables employees to direct their work, to understand what should and shouldn't be done relative to the stated aims of the organization. It helps frame decision-making and filters what matters from what does not. For example, if the vision is to maximise shareholder returns, what matters is ensuring revenues are greater than costs, while who matters is a narrow band of individuals – shareholders. Consequently, the logical implications of the vision are that costs that can be avoided and revenues that can be secured should be. So, the costs of cleaning up pollution or investing in more environmentally benign processes are, wherever possible, avoided, possibly through efforts to discourage the enactment of such laws. Likewise, wage growth is dampened, potentially through reinforcing narratives of jobs being offshored or the potential loss of jobs if wages are increased.[1] Similarly, revenues might be optimized through monopolizing customer choice. Such strategies may be considered optimal and appropriate, as the vision of the business offers the balm of justification to decision-makers. However, it is self-evident that such outcomes do little more than undermine our shared prosperity.

Alternatively, if the vision is about enabling thriving societies, new horizons open. Of course the business will continue to seek returns, but such a vision widens the aperture of possibility. By widening the aperture, the business can attract customers, employees and wider stakeholders who want to support the business, rather than it having to trap customers, employees and stakeholders into supporting it. This cuts to the core of this question, whether your business wants to succeed by enabling or limiting.

Asking if your business's vision perpetuates a world you would want to live in, while not typical is, in our view, critical, as what is the point of any business if it is not enabling such an outcome? Further, such a question is critical to the challenges we face as a society. Yet even now, too often a business's vision can be focused on itself, its competitiveness and its operational efficiency. The setting, our shared context is forgotten. However, to have a great business in an awful setting is, in the long-term, pointless.

Having set the stage, the remainder of this chapter proceeds by outlining the conceptual framing of vision, purpose, mission and values, the narrative framework that forms part of a business's mental glue. From there, discussion shifts to examples of vision statements that fall either side of the ledger. To close, guidance is provided as to how this question can be applied in your business.

FRAMING

The founders of any business are trying to solve a problem and the business is a tool to achieve that. The founders may want to make themselves wealthy – however that cannot be done in a vacuum. The source of any wealth is in society and our surroundings. Consequently, even if wealth is the hoped-for outcome of a business, the desired end, then the means is always found in solving a societal problem. Wealth is just a way of keeping score. The intention of the business should be to solve the identified problem profitably without creating a swathe of new ones. However, such intentions can often be bent out of shape as the litany of corporate scandals reminds us.

Vision is often considered alongside mission, purpose and values, albeit many businesses do not clearly delineate between these elements.[2] *Purpose* is the 'why' of the business. *Vision* is the business's utopia, its idealized outcome, its ultimate ambition. *Mission* is what the business does, its strategy and plan to pursue the vision. *Values* are how the people in the business should conduct themselves, their culture, how they should behave as they engage in the mission in pursuit of the vision. Figure 4.1 provides a framework.[3] The image on the left-hand side aims to show how the purpose, vision, mission and values form the core narrative framework of a business. The triangle is shown with the values at the apex to reinforce how these can serve as the final guide to how individuals in the business show up on a day-to-day basis, and act. Hence the purpose, vision and mission are the mental framework to guide action, the values are the final attempt to influence what turns up in any one moment. It is important to note that purpose, vision, mission and values are not monolithic, they are malleable through time, they interact and inform each other. This is reinforced through the use in the image of the double-headed arrows. Highlighting how a business both shapes and is shaping its setting is the rationale for the image on the right-hand side. This illustrates how businesses operate in a context that is, from the outside in, surroundings, society and economy. The circles' perimeters are dashed to highlight how everything interacts and there are no separate spaces.

The framework offered in Figure 4.1 is simple, logical and easy to digest, and variants of it are found in many strategy texts. However, this does not mean it is broadly applied. For many companies, statements of their purpose, vision, mission and values can be found on their websites,

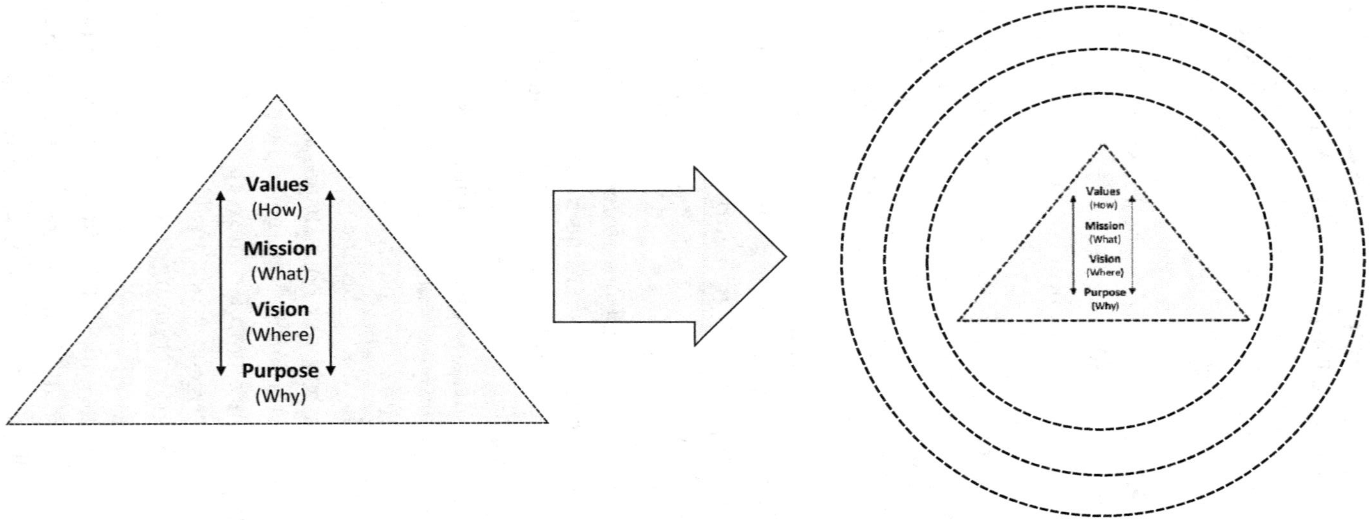

Figure 4.1 Vision, mission, purpose and values

Figures inspired by the framework put forward by the Enacting Purpose Initiative (http://enactingpurpose.org/assets/measuring-purpose--an-integrated-framework.pdf) and Collins, J. C., & Porras, J. I. (2008). CMR classics: Organizational vision and visionary organizations. *California Management Review*, 50(2), 117–137. https://doi.org/10.2307/41166438.

framed on the office wall or even reflected in their logos.[4] However, for others there may be difficulty in identifying such statements; a recent study of the values of 221 UK companies found that 14 percent did not even list them[5].

If such statements are not evident, the purpose, vision, mission and values can be distilled from conversations, a process that often reveals little to no cohesion among the business participants. We recently found this to be the case when working with different members of the senior executive group of one company. Their answers revealed a lack of common understanding and, in turn, disharmony about the why and the vision of the business. By their own admission this lack of harmony impacted operational effectiveness and efficiency, as teams were pulling in different directions. Thus, while the framework is conceptually simple and its components core to every business, applying the framework is not, it requires effort.

Turning back to the question of whether the vision of your business is perpetuating a world you want to live in. To help develop your ideas it can be useful to consider some examples that are, in our view, on opposite sides of the ledger; those that perpetuate a world you may want to live in and those that do not. Some examples are shown in Figure 4.2.

The statements were gathered from company websites, and while the statements don't fit neatly into the conceptual framing in Figure 4.1, they do highlight where the business is trying to get to. On the right-hand side of Figure 4.2 is a statement from Triodos Bank and another from Seventh Generation. These statements are offered as positive answers to the question of whether your business's vision perpetuates a world you want to live in.

Triodos Bank, as its statement highlights, wants to help create a society with human dignity at its core, while Seventh Generation aims to transform the world into a healthy, sustainable and equitable place for future generations. Both statements are constructed from the foundation of business as a tool for enabling us to live well, both now and into the future.

Alternatively, on the left-hand side of Figure 4.2 are statements offered as negative answers. For example, the JP Morgan statement highlights how it aims to be the most respected in the world in serving its customers, while the ExxonMobil statement highlights its intent to be a premier company that achieves superior results. The challenge of

JP Morgan	We aim to be the most respected financial services firm in the world, serving corporations and individuals in over 100 countries. (JP Morgan website accessed 2nd December 2022 - https://www.jpmorgan.com/about)
Exxon Mobil	Exxon Mobil Corporation is committed to being the world's premier petroleum and chemical manufacturing company. To that end, we must continuously achieve superior financial and operating results while adhering to high ethical standards. (Exxon Mobil website accessed 2nd December 2022 - https://corporate.exxonmobil.com/about-us/who-we-are/our-guiding-principles)
News Corp	News Corp is a company truly greater than the sum of its parts. Driven by passion, guided by principles and acting with purpose, we are dedicated to delivering value to our customers and our shareholders with premium products and services that inform and inspire. (News Corp website accessed 14th January 2023 - https://newscorp.com/about-news-corp/)
Triodos Bank	Triodos Bank is in business to help create a society that protects and promotes the quality of life of all its members, and that has human dignity at its core. Since 1980, we have enabled individuals, organisations and businesses to use their money in ways that benefit people and the environment.... (Triodos Bank website accessed 2nd December 2022 - https://www.triodos.com/en/about-us)
Seventh Generation	...on a mission to transform the world into a healthy, sustainable, and equitable place for the next seven generations – and beyond (Seventh Generation website accessed 2nd December 2022 - https://www.seventhgeneration.com/company)
Good Energy	Good Energy exists to power a cleaner, greener world together with our customers, generators, investors and people. (Good Energy website accessed 14th January 2023 - https://www.goodenergy.co.uk/procurement-policy/)

Figure 4.2 Some examples of visions/missions

both statements is that they put the business as the focus of what it is to prosper, be respected and recognized as pre-eminent. In this regard, both statements reinforce a perspective that business is not a tool for our prosperity, rather it is an end in and of itself. Thus, when considering the challenge question at the core of this chapter, all else being equal, these two statements are not setting forth a vision of a world where many of us would want to live. Yet while JP Morgan and ExxonMobil are in our view on the wrong side of the ledger, it is possible for them to achieve their visions while also enabling a thriving society. However, only by altering their vision statements will they give themselves permission to pursue this.

APPLYING THE QUESTION

If this chapter has done its work, it has made you reflect and consider more deeply what your business is aiming to achieve; its vision, purpose, mission and values. Not least because this question is not one that is normally asked. However, in our view, it is fundamental, as none of us exists outside of where we live.

Applying the question to your business is not easy, especially because people are generally resistant to change and seek to avoid challenges or difficult conversations. Further, those in leadership roles may be even more resistant to change as they have invested so much of themselves in pursuing the current strategic direction. They might argue that what made them successful was not challenging the status quo with such a question. Whatever the situation, the core to all change is a question and, in our experience, when asked with curiosity, such a question opens the space for conversation, reflection and movement.

Consequently, the approach we recommend would be to first capture your reflections from reading this chapter. To do this, we recommend using two key conceptual frameworks: Figure 4.1 and the being human/ wellbeing model introduced previously, now reproduced as Figure 4.3. Figure 4.1 is relevant because it reminds you of the embeddedness of the business, while Figure 4.3 offers you a framework to consider what enables human wellbeing and thus living well. Key to Figure 4.3 are the four zones, which re-situate humans into a bed of relationships, rather than consider workers as removed from all contexts. Using this model, it is important to consider how your business can support each of these zones.

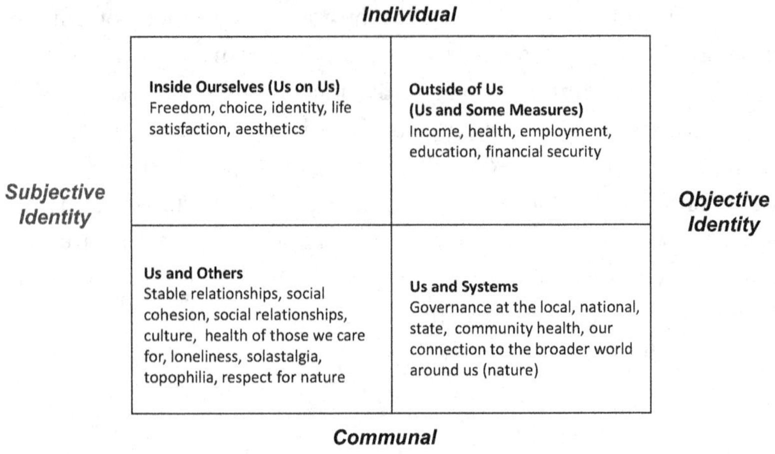

<table>
<tr><td colspan="2" align="center">*Individual*</td></tr>
<tr>
<td>

Inside Ourselves (Us on Us)
Freedom, choice, identity, life
satisfaction, aesthetics

</td>
<td>

**Outside of Us
(Us and Some Measures)**
Income, health, employment,
education, financial security

</td>
</tr>
<tr>
<td>

Us and Others
Stable relationships, social
cohesion, social relationships,
culture, health of those we care
for, loneliness, solastalgia,
topophilia, respect for nature

</td>
<td>

Us and Systems
Governance at the local, national,
state, community health, our
connection to the broader world
around us (nature)

</td>
</tr>
<tr><td colspan="2" align="center">*Communal*</td></tr>
</table>

Subjective Identity (left)   *Objective Identity* (right)

Figure 4.3 A model of being human/wellbeing revisited

Figure adapted from Painter-Morland, M., Demuijnck, G. and Ornati, S., 2017. Sustainable development and well-being: A philosophical challenge. *Journal of Business Ethics*, 146(2), pp.295-311. https://doi.org/10.1007/s10551-017-3658-4.

From here, thinking of your current vision, ask adjacent questions, such as:

- Does your vision consider impacts on society and our surroundings?
- Does your vision consider human wellbeing?
- Which aspects of the wellbeing model are enabled or hindered by the vision? For example, does it enable social cohesion or hinder it? Does it enable respect for nature or hinder it?
- Is the vision helping realize a better future for the next generation?
- What behaviours is the vision enabling? What does the current vision make permissible?
- Is the vision about the business alone or all stakeholders?

In going through this exercise, the answers may be evident or more difficult to distil. This should not be a concern, as even though a lack of clarity can be concerning, the key point at this stage is to build the initial understanding, the map. With each answer go a little further and ask: Why? Through this process it will begin to become clear what the blockers and enablers in your business are. Please note that if your business does not have a clearly written vision, write down your version of it and work from there.

Once you have completed your initial reflections the next challenge is to expand the conversation, as nothing changes in any business until you start a conversation with others. Expanding the conversation is easier said than done. Start slowly with a view to the ultimate destination being a workshop (or, more likely, a series of workshops) with relevant stakeholders. During these workshops also pose more positively framed questions such as:

- What kind of world do we want to help build?
- What are the values we wish to perpetuate?
- How do we make this business one that our children will be proud of?
- Why are we in business? What is the problem we are solving? Why does that matter?

This basic framework of apply, reflect, discuss and workshop is high-level and avoids some of the detailed challenges that you will face along the way. However, through pulling colleagues together you will enrich the discussion in your organization and enliven your business, especially if you respond to the questions with ambition and an openness to possibilities. The best visions are not necessarily achievable; they are aspirational and such aspiration is motivating for all stakeholders.

Having completed the initial workshop(s), more discussion and iteration will be required. The statements of the vision, mission, purpose and values will need to be adjusted and made concise and memorable. There is no simple way to do this; time and discussion is required. Key to this is whether your vision, mission, purpose and values can be distilled to one or two sentences that would make sense to someone you met at a party. If they require too much explanation, they will not enable you to effectively communicate with all stakeholders and they will not be as effective in their role as the narrative glue that binds your business and guides employees in their work. The statements need to be easily memorized, otherwise individuals will fill the void with their own versions. This will in turn reduce your operational efficiency and effectiveness.

To close, it is critical in our view that whenever you ask whether your business's vision is perpetuating a world in which you want to live, that you do this from a mental space that is akin to the Rawlsian original position.[6] By this we mean: ask the question with a view to whether you would be okay with the answer no matter where you were born in the world, no matter who your parents are, no matter what your gender is, no matter what your abilities. If you can answer this question from such a perspective and still your business is enabling a world you want to live in, it has a Future Normal direction. Such a direction, however, requires alignment to deliver. This is the subject of the next question: Is your business aligned with our world?

NOTES

1 This is a very common argument put forward by employer groups when the issue of raising minimum wages is discussed. In 2003 Andrew Leigh, then a scholar in the John F. Kennedy School of Government at Harvard University and now the Assistant Minister for Competition, Charities and Treasury in the Australian Federal Government, published a paper in the *Australian Economic Review* estimating the effect on employment of six increases in the minimum wage in Western Australia between 1994 and 2001. He concluded that there was a negative effect, but that it was very small – for every 1 percent increase in the minimum wage, employment fell by 0.13 percent; a result supported by the findings of a 2018 Reserve Bank of Australia discussion paper. Similarly sized effects have been found in other jurisdictions, including the United States and the United Kingdom. See: Leigh, A. (2003). Employment effects of minimum wages: Evidence from a quasi-experiment. *Australian Economic Review*, 36(4), 361-373. https://doi.org/10.1111/j.1467-8462.2003.00295.x. The Reserve Bank discussion paper can be found here: https://www.rba.gov.au/publications/rdp/2018/2018-06/full.html.

2 In defining these separate elements, we adopt the framework put forward by the Enacting Purpose Initiative, a multi-institution partnership between the University of Oxford, the University of California Berkeley, BCG BrightHouse, EOS at Federated Hermes and the British Academy. They define these elements as follows: *Purpose* articulates why an organization exits; *Values* articulate how the organization behaves; *Mission* sets out what the organization does; and *Vision* describes where the organization intends to have impact. The framework can be found here: http://enactingpurpose.org/assets/measuring-purpose---an-integrated-framework.pdf.

3 The triangle image is inspired by a seminal article in the *California Management Review* written by Jim Collins and Jerry Porras, authors of the 1994 bestselling business strategy book *Built to Last: Successful Habits of Visionary Companies*. Originally published in 1991, the article was reprinted in 2008 as part of the *California Management Review Classics* series. See: Collins, J.C., & Porras, J.I. (2008). CMR classics: Organizational vision and visionary organizations. *California Management Review*, 50(2), 117-137. https://doi.org/10.2307/41166438.

4 Businesses often focus on their vision, mission, values and purpose and finely craft these qualitative statements that are used to guide behaviors and decision-making. Alongside this, attention should be placed on the business's symbolism, for example its logo. Logos tends to be everywhere within a business – on the website, on stationary, on company vehicles, merchandise and so much more. Consequently, rather than consider a logo as just an add-on, the possibility of whether the logo can also

communicate the strategic direction of the business should be explored. One company that has done this well is Schlumberger, the engineering company. In 2022, they rebranded to become SLB and changed their logo to one that knowingly has the carbon-reduction curve within it. Thus, the logo is a visual representation of the company's purpose of creating technology that benefits all and helps their customers decarbonize. See: https://www.slb.com/about/who-we-are. Note the logo in the top left-hand corner. A Reuters article about the rebranding can be found here: https://www.reuters.com/business/energy/oil-giant-schlumberger-rebrands-itself-slb-low-carbon-future-2022-10-24/.

5 This study, conducted by the Oxford Character Project at the University of Oxford, analyses the language of websites and annual reports with respect to four main questions: What are the organizational values of UK firms? How do firms define their values? How do firms select their values? How do firms put their values into practice? The full report can be found here: https://oxfordcharacter.org/research/uk-business-values-2022.

6 John Rawls was a 21st century philosopher who sought to establish the principles of a just society. To do this Rawls employs the device of imagining a hypothetical state, the 'original position', prior to any agreement about principles of justice, the organization of social institutions and the distribution of material rewards or endowments. In this original position, individuals exist behind a 'veil of ignorance', where, for example, they are unaware of their gender, ethnicity or social status. Rawls concludes that under these circumstances, people would unanimously agree on the following fundamental principles of justice. First, the liberty principle, which establishes equal basic liberties for all. Second, the equality principle, which states that social and economic inequalities must satisfy the following conditions: a) they are attached to offices and positions that are open to all (equality of opportunity) and b) they are arranged in such a way as to be of the greatest benefit to the least-advantaged members of society (referred to as Rawls' difference principle).

Five

Aligning to deliver on the vision of a business matters. The narrative framework of the business, its vision, purpose, mission and values are only one part of the equation. Delivery requires some alignment of world view. This can be difficult as our world views have an ephemeral quality, a transience that arises from their constant evolution. Once we think we have them pinned down, they can shift. That they shift reinforces how businesses are not things, they are continual acts. Thus, change is constant and as such, ensuring a business continues in its desired direction with individuals aligned to act that way requires continual reinforcement. This idea is reinforced in Figure 5.1.

While thinking of a business as a continual act is relatively simple, this understanding can be eroded by some aspects of the English language. To explain, the English language typically deals in a form of structure that is subject then verb or action, thus a subject is invariably acting.[1] An example of how we might use this structure is to say 'the wind is blowing'. This statement denotes an understanding in us, that the subject is the wind and that this subject is performing the separate act of blowing. Yet this is not the case. When we feel the wind, we know the subject and the act are one and the same. The wind is the blowing, otherwise there is no wind. Building on this, when we consider a business is the acts it performs, it is more accurate to say 'the business is the acts', rather than 'the business acts'. Likewise, 'the business is its people' is a statement that could be more accurately refined to 'the business is the acts of its people'. This understanding, that a business emerges from its acts in the world, is the foundation upon which we understand that those acts are

DOI: 10.4324/9781003360636-7

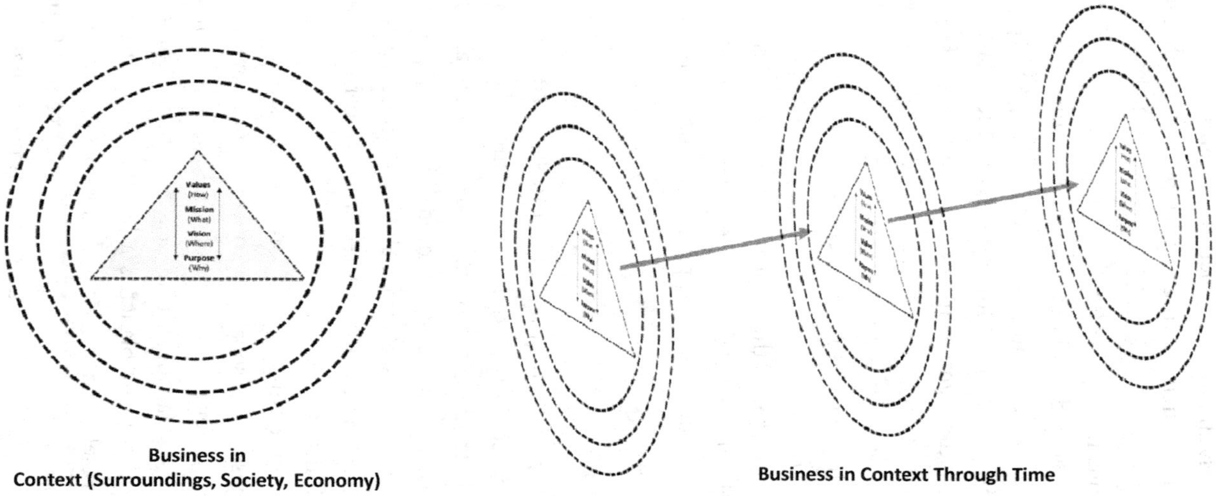

**Business in
Context (Surroundings, Society, Economy)**

Business in Context Through Time

Figure 5.1 Business in context and through time

informed by the narrative framework of the business and, importantly, the world view of the people who constitute it. From this the importance of alignment emerges. Specifically, alignment between how individuals perceive the business and how they perceive themselves, as for a business to act effectively and efficiently the gap between the individual and the business should be small. Hence, the question of this chapter comes to the fore: Is your business aligned with our world?

As we have discussed, a Future Normal business is one that acts meaningfully in our surroundings and purposefully to benefit itself and society. Ground-zero is that individuals in the business have a world view that does not separate them from their surroundings. Further, for the business to achieve its outcomes, those individuals should perceive that the business does not do this either. Uncovering this alignment, or likely misalignment, is the core of this chapter.[2]

To enable you to explore alignment in your business, this chapter proceeds by offering some theoretical framing of world views, then, some simple tools of exploration, the results of a global survey and a description of a case study. Finally, applying the question in your business is discussed.

FRAMING

A world view or paradigm (the terms can be used interchangeably) is typically considered to be a frame of meaning that is comprised of shared values, beliefs and assumptions.[3] The terms are a form of short-hand that help to emphasize a commonality of perspective within a group of people.[4] Albeit this commonality is not necessarily about complete unity of perspective, rather it tends to concern some taken-for-granted assumptions.

In Chapter 2 we outlined that conventional strategic frameworks assume the business exists separately to its surroundings and that those surroundings are independently given and without limit. However, as outlined, this is a fallacy. Businesses operate within societies and our surroundings, and our planet is a limited living space. While this understanding is self-evident, not all businesses operate with this world view and neither do all individuals. Yet to enable Future Normal outcomes, having a world view where there is no separation matters.

To have such a world view, we need to have a sense of connection to our surroundings, as we will then consider acts that degrade our surroundings as acts of self-destruction, while acts that enhance our surroundings will be considered acts of self-preservation.[5] This sense of connection is determined by the extent to which an individual includes our surroundings in their cognitive representation of themselves.[6] Thus, whether we consider our society and surroundings in our sense of self. Unfortunately, the dominant paradigm in Western societies is one of individualism, profit maximization and that we believe the path to fulfilling our wellbeing, our ultimate ends, is to buy more stuff.[7]

One method of exploring this cognitive representation of ourselves is to use detailed questionnaires and frameworks that consist of extensive sets of assumptions and values.[8] However, an alternative is to use a simple visual, non-verbal scale such as the Inclusion of Nature in Self (INS), as outlined in Figure 5.2.[9]

This scale measures our connection to nature, or as we have discussed prior, our surroundings. As illustrated, from left to right the scale moves from low to high overlap, with the numerical scale ranging from one to seven, where a score of one represents total separation and a score of seven total overlap. Thus, a person that sees themselves as separate to nature (surroundings) would score themselves a one, a person that saw themselves as connected and not separate would score themselves a seven. The INS scale can be adapted to consider how individuals view the business they work for, whether they think it operates with a strong sense of connection or not. Depicted in Figure 5.3, this is called the Inclusion of Nature in Organization (INO) scale.[10]

The INS and INO scales are tools that can be used to audit alignment between the business and its people and whether they consider the business to be operating in a manner that will enable the business to become Future Normal. A global survey[11] of 632 managers and professionals revealed that, in terms of the INS scale, individuals who scored themselves with low overlap tended to be male, executives and managers who had studied conventional strategy and had not studied beyond a bachelor's degree. Whereas those who scored themselves with higher overlap tended to be executives and managers of both genders who had studied strategy *and* sustainability. Results also revealed a general misalignment wherein, on average, individuals scored themselves higher than their organizations on the INS/INO scale. Further, individuals were of the view that their organizations needed to shift towards the right-hand side of the INO scale to operate more sustainably. Figure 5.4 presents results for the full sample, indicating that, on average, individuals

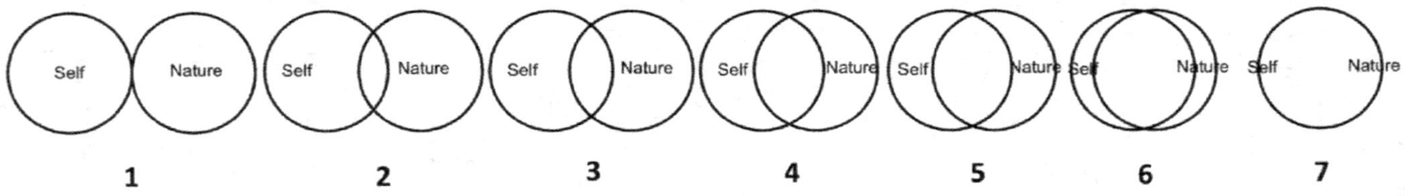

Could you please indicate which of the pictures best represents your relationship with nature? In other terms, how interconnected are you with nature? Please answer the question in terms of how you generally think/feel. There is no right or wrong answer.

Figure 5.2 The Inclusion of Nature in Self (INS) scale

Figure copied from Schultz, P.W. (2002). Inclusion with nature: The psychology of human-nature relations. In *Psychology of Sustainable Development* (pp. 61-78). Springer, New York.

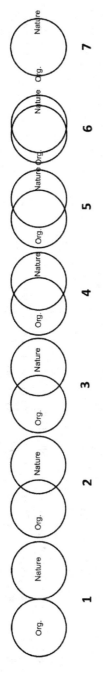

Figure 5.3 The Inclusion of Nature in Organization (INO) scale

Figure adapted from Schultz, P.W. (2002). Inclusion with nature: The psychology of human–nature relations. In *Psychology of Sustainable Development* (pp. 61–78). Springer, New York.

Could you please indicate which of the pictures best represents your view of the organization you work for and its relationship with nature? In other terms, how interconnected is the organization you work for with nature? Please answer the question in terms of how you generally think/feel. There is no right or wrong answer

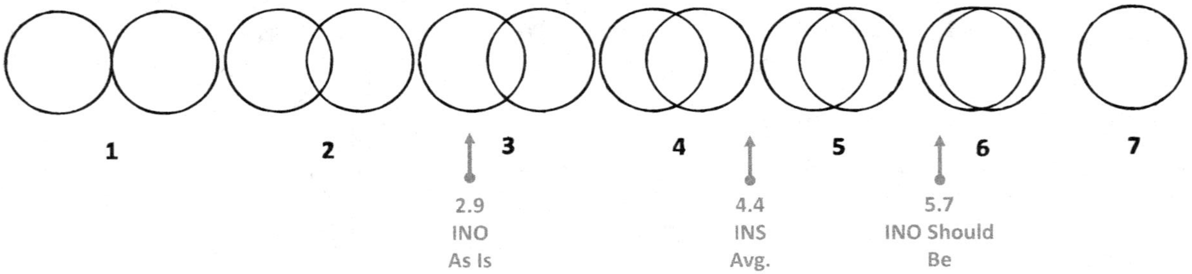

Figure 5.4 INS and INO averages, and INO ideal

Results from a global survey - Barter, N. and Alston-Knox, C., 2020. Sustainable outcomes: INS/IEO and the relevance of proximity and control to drive change. *Sustainability Accounting, Management and Policy Journal.*

scored themselves 4.4 (INS) and their organizations 2.9 (INO). Further, when individuals were asked to consider the ideal INO overlap for their organization to realize long-term, Future Normal outcomes, the average response was 5.7. Consequently, they perceived that their organization had a gap of nearly three categories between where it was and where it should be. Taken together, these results indicate that there are two significant misalignments. The first is between where individuals consider themselves and their organization to be. The second, between where their organization is and where they think it should be.

Building on this, we worked with executives from a transport company to help develop a strategy of change to shift their business to more sustainable outcomes. As part of our approach we asked the executives to score themselves and their business on the two scales, revealing scores that mirrored the results of the global survey; they scored their business lower on the INO scale than where they thought it should be by nearly three categories. Further, they judged others in the sector to be further to the right than their own business, suggesting they felt they were lagging.

While the INS and INO scales can help identify misalignment and in turn dissonance, the key challenge is that the misalignment should be narrowed. This is because such dissonance can show itself via ineffective and inefficient operations, as employees are more disengaged and less loyal because they do not see the business as keeping up with their personal world views. Further, because those same individuals tend to perceive their organization as far from ideal, this dissonance is amplified as they see a disconnect between how the business operates and how they think it should operate.

Of course, INS and INO are only diagnostic tools. Closing the gap requires developing an appropriate narrative framework (as outlined in Question One) and shifting the business's culture. Shifting culture is not easy and requires exploring world views more deeply. This can be done by considering a paradigm framework and the assumptions that comprise it, an example of which is offered in Figure 5.5. This framework is a distillation that has been shortened for ease of application. It consists of a set of nine assumptions listed under two columns, one representing old, outdated thinking and the other representing new thinking that is appropriate for our current context.[12]

As you review the framework depicted in Figure 5.5, there are key differences between the old and the new. Using this framework will allow deeper exploration beyond the results obtained from applying the

	Old 9	New 9
1. Perception of the Earth	A Dead Machine	Home
2. Humans and Our Surroundings/Nature	Separate	Entwined
3. Time Scales	Short Term	Long Term
4. Severity of Problems	Trivial	Consequential
5. Faith in Technology	Optimistic	Mixed
6. The Good Life	More Consumption	Wellbeing
7. Human Nature	Money Driven	Sapiens - More than Money
8. Role of Growth	Necessary	Mixed
9. Future Value	Much Less Important than Now	Next and Future Generations Matter

Figure 5.5 The nines framework: Old nine and new nine

Assumptions adapted from - Gladwin, T.N., Kennelly, J.J. and Krause, T.S., 1995. Shifting paradigms for sustainable development: Implications for management theory and research. *Academy of management Review, 20*(4), pp.874-907.

INS and INO scales. Consequently, using the scales in conjunction with this framework is the scaffolding you need to explore alignment in your business and in turn to shift it to one that is aligned to realize the Future Normal.

APPLYING THE QUESTION

Applying this question is relatively simple in the first instance. The first step is to survey the individuals in your team and/or the wider business and its stakeholders using the INS and INO scales presented. Ideally, we would recommend doing this at the start and then at relevant check-in times during your program of change. This will allow the results and average scores to be used as measures of change, the aim being to become more aligned towards the right-hand side of the scales. Importantly, when you conduct the surveys you should ask supplementary questions that have an open format, questions that explore respondents' rationales for their answers. For example, a supplementary question could be to ask: Why did you score that way? Or: What are the blockers and enablers preventing the business shifting to more overlap? Responses to these questions, along with the INS and INO scores, provides a richness that will enable you to develop appropriate action plans.

In the initial survey it is likely there will be misalignment, a gap between the INS, INO and INO ideal scores. We recommend sharing the results in advance of the second step, which is the more challenging work of discussion and exploration. The likelihood is that you will need to shift your business to higher overlap on the INO scale. This type of change is never easy, yet it matters as enhanced alignment reduces dissonance and encourages effectiveness and efficiency in decision-making. Such outcomes will improve business performance. To shift is the hard work of recognizing businesses are acts and culture is a movement, thus the shift relies on participative, team-based work. In turn, it relies on workshops, reflection sessions, away days, group discussion and more. In conducting these sessions, it will be necessary to explore individuals' views on the blockers and enablers of shift, as well as the components in the old nine, new nine framework. Such discussions will take time and hence shifting to alignment is not a quick fix. However, through an iterative and discursive process, the team will evermore align. This in turn may require iteration of other aspects of the business, for example those aspects discussed under each of the eight questions in the Future Normal framework.

Once new understandings have been developed and closer alignment is realized, it is important to note that constant reinforcement will be required, both through behaviors but also the metrics of performance and the wider messaging of the business. One of the key messaging devices we recommend you consider is the business's logo. Company logos are among the most pervasive imagery that stakeholders, especially employees, see. Yet there is often little concern for whether the symbol reinforces patterns of behavior your business needs to realize its Future Normal. Consequently, we recommend you conduct a review of your logo and whether it symbolizes your shift and is acting as a constant reminder.[13]

To summarize, the power of the INS and INO scales is their simplicity and how they can quickly and intuitively identify misalignment. However, understanding the reasons for the misalignment and the steps to resolve it is an involved process. Further, it is a process that once undertaken is likely to uncover other challenges across the business, perhaps its branding, perhaps its vision and purpose. Building on this, the range of overlapping circles that are the core of the INS and INO scales can also be adapted to explore individuals' alignment to, for example, the business's purpose. Where rather than label the circles 'Self' and 'Nature', the labels could be 'Individual Purpose' and 'Business

Purpose'. Alignment of individual and business purpose has been linked to employees being more loyal, engaged and willing to advocate for the business, and more willing to state that the business is having a positive impact on customers, employees, the organization and society.[14] Thus, it is possible to use the core of the INS and INO scales as a stepping stone to explore other forms of alignment.

No matter how you explore alignment, closing the gap matters and while exploration can start with some simple scales, the real challenge is that shifting is about recognizing businesses are acts and thus change is about creating a movement, not setting a mandate. This said, to whom the scales are applied can also be revealing. For example, much of the discussion in this chapter has been done within the context of employees. However, the scales and the exploration can easily be conducted with a wider set of stakeholders, including customers, suppliers and the wider community. Aligning wider stakeholders is equally useful in enabling the business to operate effectively and efficiently over the long-term. However, the consideration of who or what are relevant stakeholders expands when taking a Future Normal perspective as a business that understands it is embedded in society and our surroundings will soon realize that it needs to listen to a wider range of stakeholders. Thus, to whom the business listens is the core of the next chapter.

NOTES

1 This argument builds on that originally put forward by Tim Ingold in his 2011 book *Being Alive: Essays on Movement, Knowledge and Description*. Routledge, London.

2 Note, however, that this is not the only alignment that matters. Question Four (Chapter 7) explores the alignment required in performance measures across society, business and individuals.

3 This definition is a slightly adapted version of that offered by Minna Halme in the following article: Halme, M. (1996). Shifting environmental management paradigms in two Finnish paper facilities: A broader view of institutional theory. *Business Strategy and the Environment*, 5(2), 94-105 (see page 97). https://doi.org/10.1002/(SICI)1099-0836(199606)5:2<94::AID-BSE51>3.0.CO;2-B.

4 See: Burrell, G., & Morgan, G. (1979; reprint 2017). *Sociological Paradigms and Organisational Analysis: Elements of the Sociology of Corporate Life*. Routledge, London.

5 For further discussion see a paper Nick co-authored with Clair Alston-Knox, Senior Statistician at Predictive Analytics Group: Barter, N., & Alston-Knox, C. (2021). Sustainable outcomes: INS/IEO and the relevance of proximity and control to drive change. *Sustainability Accounting, Management and Policy Journal*, 12(1), 105-129. https://doi.org/10.1108/SAMPJ-10-2018-0275.

6 As developed by P. Wesley Schulz, see: Schultz, P.W. (2002). Inclusion with nature: The psychology of human-nature relations. In Schmuck, P., & Schulz, P.W. (eds.) (2002) *Psychology of Sustainable Development*, Springer, New York, pp. 61-78.

7 To unpack this idea further, see Lester Milbrath and Barbara Fisher's 1984 book *Environmentalists: Vanguard for a New Society*, SUNY Press, New York. An alternative source of further information is an article Nick wrote with Jan Bebbington, Rubin Chair in Sustainability in Business and Director of the Pentland Centre, Lancaster University. In this article we report the results from an empirical study that explored the views of leaders of environmentally focused organizations. See: Barter, N., & Bebbington, J. (2012). Environmental paradigms and organizations with an environmental mission. *International Journal of Innovation and Sustainable Development*, 6(2), 120-145. https://doi.org/10.1504/IJISD.2012.046945.

8 See as an example: Gladwin, T.N., Kennelly, J.J., & Krause, T S. (1995). Shifting paradigms for sustainable development: Implications for management theory and research. *Academy of Management Review*, 20(4), 874-907. https://doi.org/10.5465/amr.1995.9512280024.

9 This scale was originally developed by P. Wesley Schulz and is described in detail here: Schultz, P.W. (2001). The structure of environmental concern: Concern for self, other people, and the biosphere. *Journal of Environmental Psychology*, 21(4), 327-339. https://doi.org/10.1006/jevp.2001.0227.

10 Again see: Barter, N., & Alston-Knox, C. (2021). Sustainable outcomes: INS/IEO and the relevance of proximity and control to drive change. *Sustainability Accounting, Management and Policy Journal*, 12(1), 105-129. https://doi.org/10.1108/SAMPJ-10-2018-0275.

11 ibid.

12 These assumptions draw upon Gladwin, T.N., Kennelly, J.J., & Krause, T S. (1995). Shifting paradigms for sustainable development: Implications for management theory and research. *Academy of Management Review*, 20(4), 874-907. https://doi.org/10.5465/amr.1995.9512280024.

13 As noted in Chapter 4 (Endnote iv), one company that has done this well is SLB (formerly Schlumberger). As part of their rebranding from Schlumberger to SLB the business changed its logo to one that has the carbon-reduction curve within it.

14 As found in the 2019 McKinsey Organizational Purpose Survey and reported here: https://www.mckinsey.com/capabilities/people-and-organizational-performance/our-insights/purpose-not-platitudes-a-personal-challenge-for-top-executives#/. Further evidence is provided by, among others, multinational professional services firm EY. See: https://assets.ey.com/content/dam/ey-sites/ey-com/en_gl/topics/digital/ey-the-business-case-for-purpose.pdf.

Six

None of us thrives alone, we all rely on others to realize our goals. Those others may be near or far in time and space, and both human and non-human. For example, you may be reliant on the team you are working with right now as well as those more distant, such as the teachers who taught you to read, the engineers who built the schools you attended and the roads you drive on and so on, and so forth. Similarly, as you read this, you are reliant on those who provided you with the earnings to buy the book, but you are also reliant on non-humans; the systems that created the shared atmosphere you are breathing or the plants that created the food you are digesting or the cotton you are wearing, or the fiber for the pages of this book and so on, again almost ad infinitum. We are, as highlighted in previous chapters and depicted in Figure 6.1, embedded. Embedded in the world, embedded in the economy, in society and in our surroundings.

That none of us thrives alone also applies to business. In recent years, there have been calls for companies to embrace a broader perspective of who matters, beyond the narrow purview of shareholder primacy.[1] As discussed, the Business Roundtable of America adopted a statement in 2019 that the purpose of a corporation is to deliver value for all stakeholders,[2] with the Davos Manifesto of 2020 supporting this perspective.[3] Further, in 2022, Larry Fink, the CEO of BlackRock, one of the largest asset managers in the world, argued in his CEO letter that businesses only prosper through engaging and delivering for their key stakeholders.[4] While this widening of the aperture to include stakeholders beyond shareholders is welcome (and long overdue), the

DOI: 10.4324/9781003360636-8

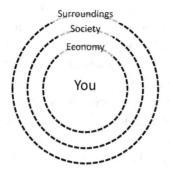

Figure 6.1 You are embedded in surroundings, society, economy

list of stakeholders commonly cited remains narrow, typically limited to shareholders, employees, customers, suppliers, regulators and the local community.

This movement in who matters, this widening of perspective to embrace more than shareholders is important. However, it only goes so far. There is still some distance to go to recognize that business success is dependent upon those near and far, human and non-human. Without further widening their perspective, business leaders will only ever be diligent in their concern for a narrow set of stakeholders, ignoring the messy complexity of the impact of their business on our wider surroundings. The Future Normal perspective widens the aperture and asks: Does your business listen to all its stakeholders?

To build the case, this chapter proceeds by offering some theoretical framing of stakeholder theory. It then extends this to a Future Normal perspective. From there, the discussiovn focusses on how to begin to shift your business so that it can more fully listen to all its stakeholders.

FRAMING

Stakeholder theory is built upon the concept that businesses should serve a range of interests, beyond shareholders, and that through aligning those wider interests they will be more successful in the long-term. The roots of the theory go back many decades, with household names such as General Electric (in 1932), Johnson and Johnson (1947)[5] and Sears (1950) all acknowledging that their stakeholders included a mix of shareholders, employees, managers, customers and the public or community.[6] The foundations of modern-day stakeholder theory, however, are more recent and can be attributed to R. Edward Freeman's 1984 book *Strategic Management: A Stakeholder Approach*. In this book, Freeman defines a stakeholder as any group or individual who can affect or is affected by the achievement of the organization's objectives.[7] In promoting stakeholder theory, Freeman argues that it helps managers make decisions based on their understanding of the world as it is today, rather than them being haunted by the past, while also allowing managers to be less internally focused and more properly consider the operating context of their business.

The central idea of stakeholder theory is that there are multiple groups who have a stake in the operation of a business, and managers should consider those groups when making decisions. That said, one of the challenges is how to define a stakeholder, as virtually everything could and can be considered. Conventionally, the response to this challenge is to narrow the stakeholders who matter by only being concerned about those that have an immediate and direct impact on the business. This approach tends to limit the business to short-term thinking and line-of-sight impacts, wherein a typical depiction of stakeholder theory is like that shown in Figure 6.2.

As illustrated in Figure 6.2, there is a limited range of stakeholders and implied equity in the power and impact of the groups surrounding the business, as illustrated through the depiction of equal sizes of and

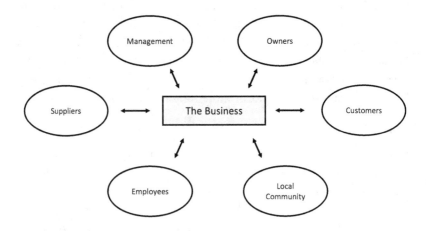

Figure 6.2 Conventional stakeholders of a business

Adapted from Freeman, R. E. (1984). *Strategic management: A stakeholder approach*. Pitman.

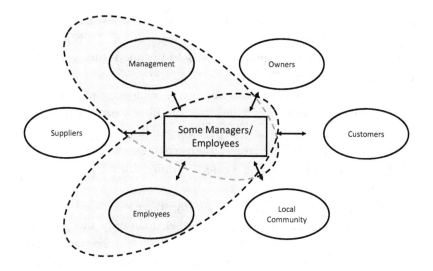

Figure 6.3 Adapted stakeholders of a business

spacing between groups, and equal sizes of arrows. This implied equity, however, quickly fails upon closer inspection. For example, managers are a sub-sample of employees and as a collection (managers and employees) are the business in the center of the image. Further, any one of us that works in a business knows that some managers or employees count more than others in terms of their influence, especially in a hierarchical structure. Consequently, a more realistic conceptualization is offered in Figure 6.3.

Building from this, while some managers and employees count more than others, so it is with owners, suppliers, customers and even communities. In turn, this brings forward the challenge of who is filtering the topics of discussion. Although filtering is unavoidable, as humans are limited beings who have biases, the task is to widen the perspective and listen to more stakeholders than convention might dictate prudent. To do this, there is a need to move beyond conventional stakeholder groupings.

The broad definition of stakeholder put forward by Freeman allows the inclusion of virtually anything, which in turn potentially renders the range of stakeholders so broad as to be unmanageable.[8] Hence, there is the question of how to identify an appropriate spectrum of stakeholders for inclusion. A focus on the now brings forward a list of stakeholders that does not just include suppliers, community, employees and alike, but also many of the natural systems that allow us to function as physical beings – for example, the air we breathe.[9] To bring in the future, a Future Normal application would include future generations as a stakeholder group. The inclusion of future generations is critically important, as they can guide the business to long-term prosperity and reflect what matters to them. Thus, they can filter a potentially infinite list of stakeholder groups to a more manageable level, as they may be more concerned about one area that impacts them rather than another. To illustrate this shift, Figure 6.4 offers a Future Normal perspective on stakeholder groupings.

Figure 6.4 builds on Figure 6.3, adding six new stakeholder groups with the final oval having no specific label, indicating the possibility for more groups. This open-ended aspect allows any business to consider its stakeholders beyond or instead of those listed, albeit all those shown matter to every business. The six additional groups are the air we breathe, the water we drink, rivers, forests, biodiversity and future generations. In bringing forward groups such as rivers and biodiversity, a first response might be to consider such groupings fantastical. However, in 2008 Ecuador changed its constitution to give nature the right to exist, flourish and evolve; in 2010 Bolivia gave nature equal rights to humans,[10] and in 2017 New Zealand passed a law to give the Whanganui River the same rights as humans[11].

Shifting from rivers and biodiversity, two critically important groups are the air we breathe and future generations. These two groupings are shaded slightly darker to reinforce their importance. Regarding the air we breathe, this grouping matters as we all share one atmosphere, and we are changing it through the burning of fossil fuels. This shift, as the IPCC has highlighted, is resulting in unprecedented changes to living conditions for all Earth's inhabitants and it is a critical issue to our shared prosperity over coming decades.

The inclusion of future generations allows us to consider longer-term impacts and help shift us from only being concerned about the now. A key concern when we consider future generations is who they are, as we often consider them to be individuals yet to be born. If we take this approach, we can tie ourselves in mental knots about how to account for them when they have no say politically or economically. Such knots can result in us justifying a form of temporal ignorance, where we willingly turn away from the future to focus on the now.

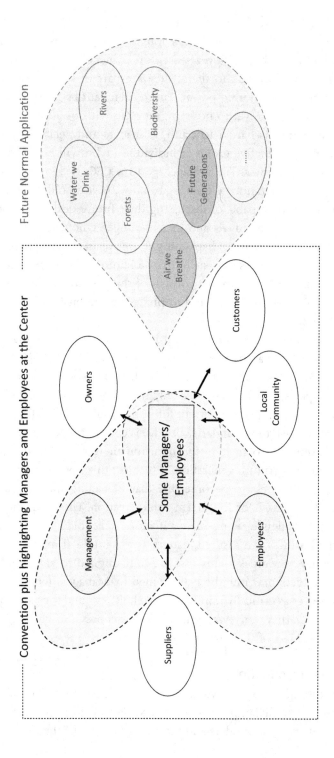

Figure 6.4 Future Normal application of stakeholder theory to a business

67   **Does your business listen to all its stakeholders?**

To facilitate a move from the abstract and unknowable to the more practical, it is useful to consider how long a generation is. The length of a generation is about 30 years;[12] future generations are here, we can account for them, talk to them, they are part of society and they have political and economic power. Future generations are no longer an abstraction of those yet to be born, they are with us. Consequently, temporal ignorance is harder to claim, as leaders and decision-makers can talk to a representative group of individuals who will be the future leaders of their business. The average age of a CEO is 56 years old.[13] Thus the future generation of leaders are now 26 years old. Such individuals are perfectly capable of discussing their future desires. Not least because it is these individuals and those younger who are particularly concerned about the changes happening to our planet through the collective actions of business.[14] As such, from a Future Normal perspective, forming a stakeholder group that consists of the potential leaders of the business in 30 years time is critical to preparing the business for long-term prosperity.

Stakeholder theory is shifting the business to listen to more than just shareholders. This is a challenge, as shareholder are owners. However, ownership does not confer inalienable rights to act without concern about the impacts on others and it is only by listening to all stakeholders that a business can position itself for long-term success. Thus, the challenge is to push the boundaries of who is considered to have a stake, beyond convention, to include the non-human (air we breathe) and the future human (future generations). In turn, this opens the door to enabling your business to become one that is leaning into its Future Normal and is geared for long-term value creation. That said, there is an additional challenge, as no matter if more stakeholders are listened to, how the business is measured matters. For example, if managers and employees have reward systems that are only aligned to shareholders, other stakeholders may only be half listened to. Managers tend to consider themselves as critically important stakeholders[15] and they are going to ensure what they do rewards them. This exposes the challenge of metrics, the subject of the next chapter.

APPLYING THE QUESTION

Applying the question of whether your business listens to all its stakeholders is both simple and complex. Simple because what has been laid out is easy to understand. Complex because of the challenges in implementation, especially because through the process of change, different arguments for and against will arise. Given this, exploring any changes to who your organization listens to would likely be a project best led by a member of your executive with supporting project-management expertise.

As with all the questions in this book, the place to start is with a conversation. That first conversation is about mapping stakeholders and working out who or what matters to the operation of the business, and why. This work is best done with a whiteboard and with reference to the first figure in this chapter, which outlines how you, all of us, and our businesses are embedded in our surroundings and society. Initially, you should produce a list of who or what you think matters to the optimal performance of your business. This will likely include simple things such as clean air and water, through to customers, suppliers and so forth. The human and the non-human will arise. From there you should go further and structure this exercise by considering the value-creation process of your business, moving from ultimate means to suppliers to operational processes to customer products and services to ultimate ends (see Chapter 3, Figure 3.2). When conducting this process, use additional questions to aid the exploration, questions such as: Where do the raw materials for the business come from? Who or what is that stakeholder? What ecosystem is impacted? What happens to the waste produced by the business? Who or what receives that? Is the waste just diluted into the air, the rivers and oceans? Is it landfilled, and if so what are the consequences for the surrounding area, for that stakeholder? In answering these questions and conducting this audit, an additional consideration is to ask: What is the business doing for each stakeholder? What is positive and what is negative? For example, paying employees could be a positive, likewise paying taxes. In contrast, efforts to reduce wages or avoid taxes negatively impact wider society. Similarly, refilling containers is positive, but if the organization is engaged in lobbying to undermine such regulations, this is a negative. Through this consideration of stakeholders and how your business is impacting them, you will get a better understanding of the signals the business is sending to all its stakeholders.

. Having worked through this initial phase of mapping stakeholders, it is likely many stakeholders who are not conventionally listened to will have been identified. Also, it is likely that the initial mapping will have been conducted internally to the business with employees and managers alone. This is appropriate, but there is a need to expand the discussion and ask those outside the business who they think the stakeholders of the business are. Also, it is assumed that, given the previous discussion in this chapter, the air we breathe and future generations have been identified as relevant stakeholders. From this initial map, the next step is to consider how best to represent different stakeholders, particularly those that have not traditionally been considered.

When considering the representation of non-human stakeholders, two options are worthy of consideration. To state the obvious, non-human stakeholders cannot speak in the conventional sense. The first method of ensuring non-human representation at stakeholder meetings is to use an empty chair. The empty chair is a signifier and an acknowledgment of, for example, the air we breathe, or a river or forest. The second method is to consider the inclusion of an appropriate specialist, for example a climate expert or an ecologist.

To focus on future generations, a shadow board could be established representing those within the business who may be leading it in 30 years' time and a mix of those who are likely to be representative of society at that time. This is to ensure that there is an appropriate level of diversity represented and the stakeholder discussions are not skewed to a particularly privileged group of individuals. Building on this, with all stakeholder groups there is a need to consider, for example, gender, ethnic and cultural diversity to ensure that a full range of voices maybe heard. From there, the challenge is to ensure that the future generations board has an appropriate mandate. When considering this mandate, it is important to consider this board as more than a method of understanding how to sell existing products to a younger age group. To date, this narrow mandate has been the convention, wherein shadow boards have been successfully used by companies to provide insights to senior executives on what younger people want.[16] Instead, the mandate should be to consider business challenges within the context of what the younger generation will inherit in time, when they are part of the leadership cadre. For example, to lean back to the first question of the core eight in this book, the remit should be one of considering the impact of current strategies and whether they are helping to create a world that the future generation will want to live in.

Exemplars can be found in the cosmetics, skin care and perfume company The Body Shop and British energy company The Good Energy. The Body Shop has formed a 'Youth Collective' of individuals under 30 years of age who the senior board of the company use to consult on business challenges,[17] while Good Energy has created a 'Good Future Board' that is staffed by six individuals who are 18 years of age or younger and whose remit is to hold the business to account on its promise of protecting their future.[18] In establishing such a board, a final consideration, no matter if it is staffed solely by younger employees in the business or include those from outside, is to ensure the psychological safety of the representatives. In reporting to a more senior board, there is an obvious challenge that those in more senior positions can be instrumental in a younger person's career and hence it is important that all participants of the board and the receivers of their messages are trained and practiced in how to both give and receive the advice shared.

Having identified a more comprehensive map of stakeholders and how they are represented, the next step is to move forward. This is the moment when the challenges may take off, as you move from the hypothetical to the practical. Given this, it is best to move forward purposefully and incrementally, as taking the business with you will take time. Setting off on this path will also bring up the challenge of measures, and whether the measures of the business and its participants are aligned, and if they enable these new conversations or not. This question is the core of the next chapter.

NOTES

1 An idea advanced by Friedman in his 1962 book *Capitalism and Freedom*, shareholder primacy is a theory in corporate governance holding that shareholder interests should be assigned priority relative to all other stakeholders.

2 Since 1978 the Business Roundtable has periodically issued statements on the principles of corporate governance. Between 1997 and 2018 all statements endorsed the principle of shareholder primacy. In a significant shift, the 2019 statement outlined what the Roundtable considered to be a modern standard for corporate responsibility, committing to deliver value to customers, invest in employees, deal fairly and ethically with suppliers, support the communities in which they work and generate long-term value for shareholders. See: https://www.businessroundtable.org/purposeanniversary.

3 Davos is the name given to the annual meeting of the World Economic Forum, after the Swiss town in which it is held. The 2020 Manifesto opens with the following statement: "The purpose of a company is to engage all its stakeholders in shared and sustained value creation. In creating such value, a company serves not only its shareholders, but all its stakeholders – employees, customers, suppliers, local communities and society at large. The best way to understand and harmonize the divergent interests of all stakeholders is through a shared commitment to policies and

decisions that strengthen the long-term prosperity of a company". See: https://www.weforum.org/agenda/2019/12/davos-manifesto-2020-the-universal-purpose-of-a-company-in-the-fourth-industrial-revolution/.

4 See: https://www.blackrock.com/corporate/investor-relations/2018-larry-fink-ceo-letter.

5 In some respects well ahead of his time, Chairman and CEO of Johnson and Johnson, Robert Wood Johnson II published the book *Or Forfeit Freedom* in 1947. In addition to his thoughts on stakeholders, Johnson argued that businesses needed to develop sustainable methods of using natural resources for the future of business and the planet. In a review of the book in the *Industrial and Labor Relations Review*, Ordway Tead, an American organizational theorist, and first president of the Society for the Advancement of Management, wrote '[Johnson's] outlook is informed, humane, practical, and morally responsible in the deepest sense.' See: Tead, O. (1948). " Or Forfeit Freedom," by Robert Wood Johnson (Book Review). *Industrial and Labor Relations Review*, 1(4), 687.

6 A more detailed history of stakeholder theory is provided by: Preston, L.E., & Sapienza, H.J. (1990). Stakeholder management and corporate performance. *Journal of Behavioral Economics*, 19(4), 361-375. https://doi.org/10.1016/0090-5720(90)90023-Z.

7 Aware that this definition was open to criticism for being too broad, Freeman argued that while stakeholder theory must be able to capture a broad range of groups and individuals, in a practical sense the strategist or manager "...must be willing to ignore certain groups who will have little or no impact on the corporation at this point in time" (p. 46). Consequently, Freeman is clear that although broad, the concept is narrowed in practical application. Further, that narrowing is based upon impact and the immediacy of that impact on the firm, not the firm's impacts on others. In this way Freeman introduces not only notions of power but also temporality into his theory.

8 An argument made by: Orts, E.W., & Strudler, A. (2002). The ethical and environmental limits of stakeholder theory. *Business Ethics Quarterly*, 12(2), 215-233. https://doi.org/10.2307/3857811.

9 We are not the first to make this argument. See for example: Starik, M. (1995). Should trees have managerial standing? Toward stakeholder status for non-human nature. *Journal of Business Ethics*, 14, 207-217. https://doi.org/10.1007/BF00881435.

10 A brief discussion of both the Ecuadorian and Bolivian cases is provided by: Berros, M.V. (2015). The constitution of the Republic of Ecuador: Pachamama has rights. *Arcadia*, 11.

11 Part of the Treaty of Waitangi settlement process between the Government of Aotearoa/New Zealand and Māori, the Te Awa Tupua (Whanganui River Claims Settlement) Act 2017 gives the Whanganui River the rights of a legal person, enabling it to do things any entity with legal personality can do, most importantly, take action to defend itself from harm. Five days after the Act was passed, India's Uttarakhand High Court granted the same legal personhood to the Ganges. See: https://www.parliament.nz/en/get-involved/features/innovative-bill-protects-whanganui-river-with-legal-personhood/.

12 In his 1960 article 'How long is a generation?' published in *The British Journal of Sociology*, Professor of Sociology, Bennett Berger, attributes consensus for the notion that a generation lasts about 30 years to Hungarian sociologist Karl Mannheim. See: Berger, B.M. (1960). How long is a generation? *The British Journal of Sociology*, 11(1), 10-23. https://doi.org/10.2307/587038.

13 Based upon analysis of 4,747 companies in the Refinitiv database undertaken in collaboration with colleague Dr Akihiro Omura in December 2021.

14 The rise of eco-anxiety in young people is well documented. For example, an article published in *The Lancet Planetary Health* reports the results of a survey of 10,000 children and young people (aged 16–25 years) in ten countries (Australia, Brazil, Finland, France, India, Nigeria, Philippines, Portugal, the UK and the USA). Data were collected on participants' thoughts and feelings about climate change, and government responses to climate change. The findings of this survey are as follows: Respondents across all countries were worried about climate change (59% were very or extremely worried and 84% were at least moderately worried). More than 50% reported each of the following emotions: sad, anxious, angry, powerless, helpless and guilty. More than 45% of respondents said their feelings about climate change negatively affected their daily life and functioning, and many reported a high number of negative thoughts about climate change (e.g., 75% said that they think the future is frightening and 83% said that they think people have failed to take care of the planet). See: Hickman, C., Marks, E., Pihkala, P., Clayton, S., Lewandowski, R.E., Mayall, E.E., ... & van Susteren, L. (2021). Climate anxiety in children and young people and their beliefs about government responses to climate change: a global survey. *The Lancet Planetary Health*, 5(12), e863-e873. https://doi.org/10.1016/S2542-5196(21)00278-3.

15 For further exploration of what or who matters to managers, at least in the context of the United States, see: Posner, B.Z. (2010). Values and the American manager: A three-decade perspective. *Journal of Business Ethics*, 91, 457-465. https://doi.org/10.1007/s10551-009-0098-9.

16 An article in the *Harvard Business Review* by Jennifer Jordan and Michael Sorell provides a discussion of the conventional use of shadow boards: https://hbr.org/2019/06/why-you-should-create-a-shadow-board-of-younger-employees.

17 For further information about The Body Shop's Youth Collective, see: https://www.thebodyshop.com/en-au/about-us/activism/beseenbeheard/our-youth-collective/a/a00076.

18 For further information about Good Energy's Good Future Board, see: https://www.goodenergy.co.uk/the-good-future-board/.

Seven

What gets measured gets done; if you can't measure it, you can't monitor it. Choose your saying – when it comes to metrics, we all have one. Understanding metrics (or measures, we will use the terms interchangeably) matters, because they drive behavior, expectations and perceptions of success. Leaders manage and motivate to drive actions that they believe will affect the metric against which they are being judged. Hence, a monetary measure drives one set of behaviors, a measure of purpose, another set.[1]

The target, the hurdle rate, is also critical. Too high and it can demotivate or drive behaviors that are aimed at 'gaming' the system, while undermining confidence in leaders who set such unrealistic targets. Too low and the targets might be considered easily achievable and thus demotivating, while again undermining confidence in leadership. Targets need to be neither too high nor too low; the golden mean needs to be found, achievable but only with appropriate effort. Figure 7.1 provides an overview of the dynamics of metrics, actions and targets.

Having set the metrics and their associated targets, at the end of the designated period results are counted and judgements made. The outcome will result in feelings of success or failure, and in turn this will lead to the story that is told. Success will be aligned with a story that reinforces the actions taken, whereas failure will be accompanied by a story of the shortcomings of others. We keep success close and push failure away.

Consequently, every measure is merely the tip of an iceberg that has beneath its surface a plethora of human behaviors, feelings and expectations. Nowhere is this more evident than in the key measure of business; money. This is the one metric that is monitored by all businesses,

DOI: 10.4324/9781003360636-9

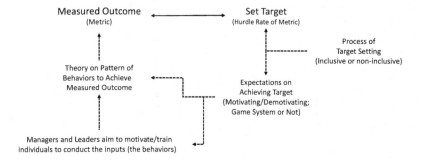

Figure 7.1 Metrics and targets

yet making it is a simple equation; sell things for more than they cost. The simplicity of this equation and its drivers are captured in Figure 7.2.

As Figure 7.2 indicates, the key to increasing returns is to increase revenue and/or decrease costs. So simple, yet there are limited ways in which to do this. To increase revenue, a business can either increase price or volume. To increase price, it has the option of segmenting the market to sell the same product at a higher price to different demographics or in different locations, or it can increase the price for all and find a strategy to ensure that customers have no choice but to continue to purchase. To increase volume, the business can get existing customers to buy more, or find new customers.

On the cost side, strategies include lowering wages (for example, by moving tasks off-shore to lower-wage countries), avoiding regulations, and sourcing lower cost materials. All these actions enable the pursuit of increased returns, and all are logical if the metric of the business is to make money and no concern is given to how that money is made. In this scenario, business behaviors are aimed at achieving monetary targets and reaping the associated rewards with little or no concern for unintended consequences.

The challenge for a business that wants to become Future Normal is to be about more than money and to see money as a means not an end. It is about the business purposefully contributing to society, acting meaningfully in our surroundings and making money. Financial return does not have to be sacrificed in the pursuit of these other outcomes. However, measures must be adjusted to align with the broader purpose. On its own, money is not a great measure of success, because we all know it is possible to be wealthy and have poor wellbeing, be

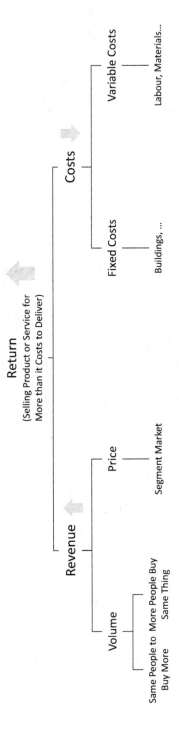

Figure 7.2 Making money: A simple algorithm

a wealthy country and have poor societal outcomes[2] and be a wealthy firm in a fragmented and dysfunctional setting. The challenge of being about more than money is that it adds complexity, whereas being about money alone is simple and comforting. It is an easy equation, revenue up and costs down, and if we stick to the equation there is no need to extend any moral reasoning beyond the bounds of the equation. Thus, complexity can be avoided and life can be simple as we are able to dismiss damage to humans, our society, or our surroundings as the concern of others.

However, our societies and the surroundings in which we are embedded and which future generations will inherit are more than money, not least because we all put value on things that are more than money. The simple question we often ask is: If your house was on fire, what would you save? Or: Name the three things that are most important to your wellbeing and happiness. The answer is seldom a list of items that can be purchased. Hence, to be a Future Normal company there is little choice but to embrace the complexity of more than money.

This chapter proceeds by offering some framing that covers broad systems and frameworks of measurement at a societal and business level, frameworks that are about more than money. This includes the United Nations (UN) Human Development Index (HDI), the Organization for Economic Cooperation and Development (OECD) Better Life Index, the Sustainable Development Goals (SDGs), Integrated Reporting, and Environmental, Social and Governance (ESG) measures. Having introduced these measurement frameworks, the process of how to apply the understanding gained to your business is outlined. Finally, some closing considerations on intrinsic and extrinsic motivation are offered, as well as some potential metrics that you might consider. The aim being to move ever closer to aligning the metrics across the different scales of individual, business and society, as illustrated in Figure 7.3.

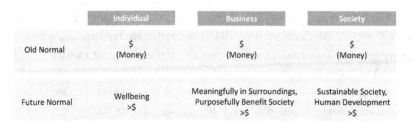

Figure 7.3 Metrics alignment: Old normal, Future Normal

The Great Depression (1929–1933) exposed shortcomings in the information available to governments to help them manage their economies. In response, the United States Department of Commerce commissioned the development of a set of national economic accounts, of which GDP is the most prominent. GDP is the total monetary or market value of all the finished goods and services produced within a country's borders in a specified period of time. Simon Kuznets, who led the development of GDP, warned at the time that such accounts were not a good measure of the welfare of a nation, as so much in life does not have an observable monetary value; parental care or clean air being obvious examples. Unfortunately, Kuznet's warning did not stop GDP being widely adopted as a proxy measure of a country's progress in much mainstream economic and political discourse.

More recently the UN and the OECD, among others, have noted that although for much of the twentieth century there was an assumption that growth in a nation's GDP aligned to progress for its citizens, this assumption is now frayed and there is a need to consider new, more holistic, measures of progress. This recognition is not new; the country of Bhutan has measured its progress by Gross National Happiness for many decades.[3] These new measures of progress are the HDI for the UN and, for the OECD, the Better Life Index.[4] The HDI aims to highlight that people and what they are capable of is key to the development of a country. It consists of three dimensions (a long and healthy life, knowledge and a decent standard of living) and four indicators (life expectancy, mean and expected years of schooling, per capita gross national income). The OECD Better Life Index operates in a similar vein, although it is more complex (11 domains and 24 indicators) and includes fewer countries (41 compared to 195). Both the HDI and the Better Life Index highlight that the success of a country is about more than money; it is about how we live.

Outside of the HDI and the Better Life Index, another set of measures are the UN SDGs. Adopted in 2015, the SDGs are framed as a universal call to action to end poverty, protect the planet and ensure that by 2030 all people enjoy peace and prosperity. As shown in Figure 7.4, there are 17 goals that can be grouped into the three domains of economy, society and planetary limits. Businesses the world over are increasingly committing to helping achieve the SDGs, with the two most supported by business being 'Goal 13: Climate Action' and 'Goal

8 – Decent Work and Economic Growth		
9 – Industry, Innovation and Infrastructure		Economy
12 – Responsible Consumption and Production		
10 – Reduced Inequalities		

1 – No Poverty	7 – Affordable and Clean Energy	
2 – Zero Hunger	11 – Sustainable Cities and Communities	
3 – Good Health and Well-Being	16 – Peace, Justice and Strong Institutions	Society
4 – Quality Education	17 – Partnerships for Goals	
5 – Gender Inequality		

6 – Clean Water and Sanitation	
13 – Climate Action	Planetary
14 – Life below Water	Limits
15 – Life on Land	

Figure 7.4 Overview of the Sustainable Development Goals (SDGs)

Image adapted from The SDGs Wedding Cake - https://www.stockholmresilience.org/research/research-news/2016-06-14-the-sdgs-wedding-cake.html and Costanza, R., McGlade, J:, Lovins, H. and Kubiszewski, I., 2014. An overarching goal for the UN sustainable development goals. *Solutions*, 5(4), pp.13-16.

8: Decent Work and Economic Growth'. In contrast, the two least supported are 'Goal 1: No Poverty' and 'Goal 14: Life Below Water', perhaps signaling where business considers their primary responsibilities to lie.[5]

Moving from these macro-level indicators, methods of accounting for business beyond the financial have been developed. Broadly these developments can be captured under the nomenclature of social and environmental accounting.[6] One of the enduring frameworks within this canon, that is easy to grasp, is the triple bottom line. First proposed by John Elkington,[7] this framework posits that a business should consider its financial bottom line, its social bottom line and its environmental bottom line. More recently, Integrated Reporting has emerged as an alternative framework,[8] expanding beyond the purely financial by asking a business to consider how it creates value across six capitals: (1) financial, (2) manufactured, (3) intellectual, (4) human, (5) social and relationship, and (6) natural. Figure 7.5 illustrates examples of the components of the six capitals and potential metrics that a business might consider within them.

Building a reporting framework on the back of a premise that the world can be divided into different capitals has been posited within

Financial

- Funds available to the business to produce its goods and services ...

Potential Measures
- Standard financial metrics

Manufactured

- Manufactured objects that the business uses to produce its goods and services can include buildings, equipment and infrastructure...

Potential Measures
- Quality, quantity, utilisation...

Intellectual

- Intellectual property and tacit knowledge such as competencies and procedures...

Potential Measures
- Patents, research projects, number of new products, ...

Human

- Alignment to the business' strategy, business loyalty...

Potential Measures
- Trust, loyalty, INO/INS scales, living wage, ...

Social and Relationship

- Shared norms, brand reputation, social licence to operate...

Potential Measures
- Trust, great place to work, INS/INO scales, customer loyalty, Net Promoter Score...

Natural

- Renewable and non-renewable resources – air, water, land, biodiversity, ...

Potential Measures
- Carbon footprints, biodiversity impact, water footprints, ...

Figure 7.5 Overview of the Integrated Reporting Six Capitals

Content adapted from Integrated Reporting Framework 081922 – downloaded from https://www.integratedreporting.org/international-framework-downloads/ on the 16 January 2023.

sustainability and business discussions for many decades.[9] The argument is that this approach has allowed nature, in the broadest sense, to be discussed in the boardroom in a language with which businesses are familiar. However, the premise of splitting the world into different capitals should not be considered without caution. Key to this caution is that the use of capitals as a master metaphor can open logics where we consider everything as a form of economic calculus. For example, we can start to shift towards considering everything as an economic transaction that can be priced. Thus, we can reduce society, ourselves and our surroundings to things that are akin to financial instruments that can earn returns, be liquidated at the right price and/or held on deposit. So much of life fails this type of calculus. For example, as an extreme, a price on oxygen could imply a logic that it would be economically rational to reduce its supply, as a shortness of oxygen would be a key enabler to ensuring a higher price is paid for the next breath. Hence using capitals as a framework should only be done with caution, with the implied logics not stretched too far.[10]

Moving from Integrated Reporting, another framework that is increasingly popular is ESG measures. These are investor-led metrics that have surged in popularity since 2005, particularly as investors have become more concerned about the impacts of a business on society and our surroundings.[11] There is a range of ESG data providers, and the market is yet to consolidate and be regulated around standard metrics. This makes consolidated views on the ESG performance of individual companies difficult, as one analysis might offer an ESG score that is markedly different from another.[12] Nevertheless, the growth of ESG measures continues.[13]

In terms of specific measures, while not limited to the following, the 'E' tends to cover areas such as emissions, pollution, environmental management policies and elements of resource efficiency; the 'S' areas such as workforce metrics, fair competition practices and human rights; and the 'G' areas such as shareholder protection, whether the business is aligned to any of the SDGs and board diversity. In all, there are more than 500 different measures, split relatively evenly across the three domains.[14] This raises many challenges in interpretation, which is not helped by the way many measures are constructed. For example, it is common for a 'yes/no' metric to be employed. That is: Does the company have a particular policy in place, 'yes' or 'no'? This does not yield any insight into the effectiveness or ambition of the policy. Alternatively, a metric may be numerical – for example, the percentage of female board members.

While more revealing than a 'yes/no' metric, in isolation it reveals little, leading to the need for industry benchmarking or analysis of trends over time.

A further challenge with ESG is that it is often conflated with sustainability. Such conflation is misguided, as sustainability arises from a societal perspective, whereas ESG is from an investor perspective. Likewise, sustainable development concerns future generations and stewardship, something that is not central to ESG. Thus, even though ESG and sustainability can overlap, they are distinct concepts. This situation is reinforced through an opaqueness regarding how different ESG metrics are developed and how they link to sustainable outcomes, such as those within SDG targets. Nevertheless, while there is an unevenness in ESG growth, with Europe leading the USA,[15] ESG investments continue to grow, enabling businesses, particularly as they search for more loyal investors[16], to discuss and explore what it means to develop a business that acts with more consideration to society and our surroundings.

Having introduced a range of metrics and frameworks, the challenge is to distil this broad understanding and apply it to your business. Such an application will allow your business to set targets and expectations, backed up by appropriate measurement, on its path towards becoming Future Normal.

APPLYING THE QUESTION

Key to any system of monitoring and measuring the performance of a business is ensuring efficient and effective alignment to the business' purpose, vision and mission. Efficient meaning the actions being taken are done well, effective meaning those actions are the right things to achieve. That said, it is important to note that any alignment is partial and temporary. It will require periodic review, particularly because the operating context for any business is continually changing and, in turn, so are the demands and expectations of stakeholders.

Taking alignment and its temporal nature as a starting point, the process of developing the right metrics to become a Future Normal business, as with all the questions in this book, begins with a conversation. This conversation should proceed through the stages of identifying potential metrics, distilling their range and how best to achieve their implementation and iteration.

Drawing on the range of frameworks discussed above, identifying potential metrics involves engaging with stakeholders and experts. Also, in appreciating the business is embedded, it should become evident that the business impacts society and our surroundings, and this in turn will draw out some logical metrics of impact and success. Engagement with stakeholders is about exploring what success looks like for the business from their perspective. In so doing, it is important to add a temporal element to this conversation, discussing with stakeholders what will matter over the next five, ten and 30 years. These conversations will take time and a long list of metrics will likely be identified.

The second stage is to distil the range of metrics. Doing this is ultimately a judgement call, there is no perfect metric or range of metrics, rather there will be a range that matter to your business. In making these judgements, a key parameter is alignment to strategic direction and actionability. Actionability concerns which metrics can be influenced by management's actions. In essence, which metrics the business can shift the needle on.

The third stage, implementation, consists of many aspects, including information systems for reporting, engaging with stakeholders and target setting. When considering the latter, the expectation management associated with target setting is, as outlined earlier, critical. In turn, the translation of the measures and targets to individual performance frameworks is key, as what is incentivized will get done. The range of metrics distilled to help the business become Future Normal will include a range of financial and non-financial measures, and the targets and rewards associated with their achievement will drive behaviors. Regarding rewards, it is important to consider that not everyone is extrinsically motivated, and excessive monetary rewards can erode an individual's desire to do the right thing, as well as arousing feelings of hubris that can result in them engaging in excessive risk taking and developing a short-term focus.[17] Whereas, working for a purposeful company can be inspiring and potentially motivating for employees in and of itself.[18] As such, there is a balance to be found, a balance that again relies on judgement.

Having identified the range of metrics, distilled and implemented them, the fourth stage is iteration. This is about recognizing that the metrics appropriate for now will likely shift and change in time as the business and its operating context evolves. Hence the need to recognize that periodic conversations with stakeholders will be required.

While a four-stage process is easy to explain, it can be difficult to get started. To aid this, some metrics beyond financial that could be

Surroundings

- Non-renewable resource use relative to renewable resource capacity
- Greenhouse gas emissions and their alignment to science based targets
- Days of clean, healthy air in vicinity of the business' operations (consider this the inverse of air pollution)
- Drinkability of the business's liquid outputs, is it benign?
- Whether the solid waste of the business could be stored in locally, is it benign?
- Number of earths it would take to support the business, if every business operated as it does now.
- The estimated cost of the externalities produced by the business
- Ecological footprint of the business
- Is the business biodiversity positive?
- Amount of materials reused
- ...

Society

- Diversity, Equity and Inclusion metrics
- Community engagement
- Taxes paid
- Wellbeing of employees, suppliers and local community
- Living wage relative to local society
- Pay ratio between executives and lowest paid
- Employee loyalty
- Customer loyalty
- ...

Business

- Standard financial metrics
- Governance structures including a future generation board
- Stakeholder representation including non-human stakeholders
- ...

Figure 7.6 Metrics that could be considered

List of metrics is inspired by the authors' consulting projects, research experience and Daly, H.E., 2014. *Beyond Growth: The Economics of Sustainable Development.* Beacon Press and Meadows, D., 1998. Indicators and information systems for sustainable development. In *The Earthscan Reader in Sustainable Cities* (pp. 364-393). Routledge.

considered for a Future Normal business are highlighted in Figure 7.6. Although not comprehensive, the metrics shown provide a perspective on what businesses could measure beyond money.

Penultimately, as you consider the content of this chapter, an overarching challenge is that developing the metrics for a Future Normal business is a process that increases complexity. This is necessarily so, the days of not being concerned about the impact of a business on society and its surroundings are past.

To close, having identified a more comprehensive set of metrics and having worked through setting a new vision (question one), developing alignment (question two) and listening to new stakeholders (question three), the next challenge is to begin to consider the 'how' of the business. This is the territory of the next four questions, which consider how the business talks to itself, its footprint, its production processes and how it shows up relative to others.

NOTES

1 An article discussing the metrics that CEOs consider when measuring purpose, based on data from the 2022 Brandpie CEO Purpose Report, can be found here: https://www.brandpie.com/thinking/evolving-purpose-measures.

2 This is a key insight of the UN HDI. The HDI reveals that nations with similar levels of wealth can have vastly different human development outcomes. For example, in the 2021 Index, Norway and the United States had very similar gross national income per capita (64,660, ranking 8th and 64,765, ranking 7th respectively), yet Norway had a much stronger HDI score (ranking 2nd with a score of 0.961 compared to 21st with a score of 0.921). Another example is Laos and Vanuatu, both have HDI scores of 0.607 (equal 40th) yet Laos' gross national income per capita is over double that of Vanuatu (7,700, ranking 128th compared to 3,085, ranking 163rd). Human development, therefore, is clearly not just about a nation's level of wealth. All income figures are in 2007 dollars adjusted for purchasing power parity. See: https://hdr.undp.org/data-center/human-development-index#/indicies/HDI.

3 A term first coined by the King of Bhutan in 1972, Gross National Happiness strongly influences Bhutan's economic and social policy. The Gross National Happiness Index consists of nine domains ranging from psychological wellbeing to ecological diversity and resilience. Constructed via 33 indicators, the Index groups people into unhappy, narrowly happy, extensively happy, or deeply happy. See: https://www.grossnationalhappiness.com/.

4 See Chapter 2 for further discussion.

5 As indicated by public disclosure of support, as compiled and reported by United States-based finance company MSCI. See: https://www.msci.com/who-cares-about-the-un-sustainable-development-goals.

6 In his 2014 article, Professor Lee Parker provides an in-depth overview of the development of social and environmental accounting since its inception in the 1980s until recent times. See: Parker, L. (2014). Constructing a research field: A reflection on the history of social and environmental accounting. *Social and Environmental Accountability Journal*, 34(2), 87-92. https://doi.org/10.1080/0969160X.2014.938472.

7 While Elkington first coined the term in 1994, his 1998 article published in the journal *Measuring Business Excellence* provides the first clearly documented overview of the concept. See: Elkington, J. (1998). Accounting for the triple bottom line. *Measuring Business Excellence*, 2(3), 18-22. https://doi.org/10.1108/eb025539.

8 The Integrated Reporting Framework and companion documents can be found here: https://www.integratedreporting.org/resource/international-ir-framework/.

9 See for example: Lovins, A.B., Lovins, L.H., & Hawken, P. (1999). A road map for natural capitalism. *Harvard Business Review*, 77, 145-161.

10 For further discussion see: Barter, N. (2016). A review of "A New Vision of Value" – old wine, new bottle. *Sustainability Accounting, Management and Policy Journal*, 7(4), 531-538. https://doi.org/10.1108/SAMPJ-12-2015-0111. And: Barter, N. (2015). Natural capital: dollars and cents/dollars and sense. *Sustainability Accounting, Management and Policy Journal*, 6(3), 366-373. https://doi.org/10.1108/SAMPJ-02-2014-0011.

11 For a recent overview of the ESG landscape, see: https://www.mckinsey.com/capabilities/sustainability/our-insights/does-esg-really-matter-and-why#/.

12 A discussion of this issue and others is provided in a recent review of responsible investing conducted by colleagues of ours at the Griffith Business School. See: Fan, J.H., Omura, A., & Roca, E. (2022). An industry-guided review of responsible investing: Bridging the divide between academia and industry. *Journal of Cleaner Production*, 354, 131685. https://doi.org/10.1016/j.jclepro.2022.131685.

13 According to a 2022 report from global professional services firm PWC, ESG investment is predicted to soar, making up a little over 20% of all assets under management by 2026. See https://www.pwc.com/gx/en/industries/financial-services/asset-management/publications/asset-and-wealth-management-revolution-2022.html.

14 This estimate of the number of ESG measures is based on research employing the Refinitiv database conducted in June 2022 with a colleague, Dr Akihiro Omura.

15 Addisu Lashitew, a non-resident fellow at The Brookings Institution (a nonprofit public policy organization based in Washington, DC) argues that the United States and Europe are taking divergent paths regarding ESG, with the United States taking a more lenient, less regulated approach, leaving investors with less confidence in the ESG claims being made. See: https://www.brookings.edu/blog/future-development/2021/09/28/the-risks-of-us-eu-divergence-on-corporate-sustainability-disclosure/.

16 There is evidence to suggest ESG investors are more loyal: See Fan, J.H., Omura, A., & Roca, E. (2022). An industry-guided review of responsible investing: Bridging the divide between academia and industry. *Journal of Cleaner Production*, 354, 131685. https://doi.org/10.1016/j.jclepro.2022.131685.

17 As discussed in an article in the Financial Times Moral Money Forum. See: https://www.ft.com/content/d4aedc19-93c4-4fee-ae51-acac48ed13b7.

18 A 2020 article published in *Frontiers in Psychology* reports the results of an empirical test of the association between purpose and employee motivation and engagement for a Dutch multi-national company. The results find a positive association between purpose and employee motivation and engagement but only a causal relationship between purpose and engagement, not motivation. In addition to reporting the results of their analysis, the article provides a comprehensive overview of existing literature. See: van Tuin, L., Schaufeli, W.B., Van den Broeck, A., & van Rhenen, W. (2020). A corporate purpose as an antecedent to employee motivation and work engagement. *Frontiers in Psychology*, 11, 572343. https://doi.org/10.3389/fpsyg.2020.572343.

Question Five: Does your business use language that enables?

Eight

To say language matters is perhaps too obvious a statement. Language guides how we think and act. This is particularly true in businesses, where because they are intangible; we use language to make them intelligible, understood and actionable.[1] There is a plethora of advice on language for business, be that the language to use for your brand, your advertising, your leadership, your media releases or your vision. This chapter, however, is not about advice in any of those specific areas. Rather, it explores language in two distinct ways. By first discussing how metaphors pervade business language and the challenges this may provoke, and second, how we can use language to decrease psychological distance and inspire action.

Metaphors populate our language. We all know some simple everyday metaphors that are applied in our organizations, many of which evoke images of sport, such as 'cover your bases', 'stepping up to the plate' and 'being on the ball', or war, such as 'making a killing', 'outflanking the competition' and 'rallying the troops'.[2] The use of metaphors enables us to enhance our understanding of the world by facilitating our conception of one thing in terms of something else. Thus, they are a mental shortcut that can be a catalyst to thinking about a challenge in a new way. This strength of metaphors, however, is also their weakness. This chapter explores this weakness in the context of two common metaphors used in business: business as a machine and business as an organism.[3]

To further highlight how metaphors perpetuate behaviors, a prescient example is the 'Community Game, Wall Street Game' study.[4] Two experiments were conducted, one with American college students and one with Israeli Air Force pilots and their instructors. In both

DOI: 10.4324/9781003360636-10

experiments, participants were split into two groups and presented with the same classic prisoner's dilemma scenario. The prisoner's dilemma is a simple co-operation game used in economics to explain why individual incentives might lead actors to choose a sub-optimal outcome.[5] In one group, participants were told they were playing the 'community game', the other group the 'Wall Street game'. In both the college and air force experiments, those playing the 'community game' were significantly more likely to co-operate than those playing the 'Wall Street game'. The metaphorical framing mattered.

Turning to psychological distance, key to enabling us to act in ways that result in better outcomes for society and our surroundings is that we have a sense of connection.[6] This sense of connection is built upon a logic that we need, for example, to see degradation in our surroundings and society as an act of self-destruction to prompt a change in our behavior. Likewise, we need to see improvement of our surroundings and society as improvement in self. A simple everyday example of this is that the individuals who live near an industrial site that pollutes are greater advocates of clean up relative to those that don't.[7] That said, this chapter does not discuss the challenge of whether individuals live close to a problem, rather it is about how we can adjust language to reduce psychological distance and inspire action. For example, is the challenge gaseous emissions in the atmosphere or the quality of the air we breathe?

To build a case regarding these two aspects of language and to enable the challenge question of this chapter to be explored, the chapter proceeds by first framing some theory regarding metaphors before discussing the implications of the machine and organism metaphors specifically. From there, theory regarding psychological distance is brought forward and the results of a study regarding phraseology that collapsed psychological distance and implied action are presented. From this foundation, how to apply the lessons of this chapter to your business is outlined.

FRAMING

Metaphors have been likened to viruses that spread meaning and guide our perceptions, allowing us to connect our experiences to our imaginations.[8] They are entwined in the relationship between thought, meaning and action with the metaphor implying a mode of behavior. Consequently, metaphors are akin to a cognitive technology that shapes our relationship with our surroundings and guides how we think and act.[9] In this way, they are self-fulfilling prophecies for how we ascribe the functioning of reality, and it this ability that makes the use of any single metaphor challenging, especially because they involve the transfer of a way of thinking from a familiar, to a new, domain.[10] This transfer from the familiar to the new involves us making inferences about things we may know little about, upon the basis of another thing, we may know something about. Metaphors, therefore, are a form of shorthand. However, as with all shorthand solutions, they need a 'user beware' sticker attached. For example, one metaphor that has been argued as being at the root of modern human understanding is 'The Great Chain of Being'.[11] This chain places humans on a scale that we are at the top of, relative to other forms of life such as animals and plants. This self-aggrandizement is nice for us, but it has little connection to how we evolved. Hence, while it is a metaphor that we can use about ourselves to reinforce our importance, it removes us from fully considering how we are within and part of our surroundings. Further, it promotes a perspective that our progress is reducible to the survival of the fittest and, as such, our context is something we need to compete or be at war with.

Turning to language in business, a challenge regarding convention is that the language of strategic decision-making is writ large with war-like metaphors. This comes forward in simple ways. For example, an ancient Chinese military treatise, Sun Tzu's *The Art of War*, is a common supporting text when teaching strategy,[12] and strategic language is replete with terms such as 'target', 'capture', 'defend', 'deploy' and 'campaign'[13]. This language reinforces the notion that a business should continually operate with a heightened state of awareness as it is subject to potential attack at any time.[14] In turn, this translates to the behavior of business. Yet this could be different; as if alternative metaphors were commonplace, so would alternative business behaviors[15].

Two common metaphors used for business to help our understanding of them are machine and organism. These two metaphors are at the tip of something greater regarding symbolism and association. For example, the machine metaphor draws upon mechanics, notions of economic rationality, hierarchy, efficiency, the business being closed off and how the humans that constitute the business should be considered as little more than functional parts. Consequently, the machine metaphor promotes a view of business that humans are only useful in so much as they enable the continued operation of the machine. This situation privileges the business, an abstract that exists as an inter-subjective idea, relative to the humans that constitute it. As such the use of the machine metaphor reduces humans to cogs in a machine, the wellbeing of which is demoted relative to the success of the business. In short, the machine metaphor perpetuates a perspective that the business is what matters, and it holds priority over us and our wellbeing. Hence, we trap ourselves into defining everything relative to the business, privileging it and putting it into competition with us. Thus, rather than the business adapting and innovating to enable great outcomes for all, the machine metaphor traps business decision-makers into pitting the ongoing mode of operation of the business against the best interests of society and our surroundings.[16]

The organism metaphor also raises concerns. These range from the implication that the business has a life of its own beyond that of its human constituents, to the demotion of humans to little more than functional parts of the organism. This demotion is like that implied by the machine metaphor, and again results in an elevation of the needs of the business relative to all else. Thus, to enable a business to thrive, our context must be manipulated to fit the requirements of that business. This perpetuates the notion that a business can be separated from us, our society and our surroundings – a fallacy.

In addition to summarizing the challenges of the machine and organism metaphors, Figure 8.1 highlights the challenges of the term 'human resources' and the visual metaphor of Michael Porter's five forces.[17]

Turning to psychological distance, this concerns how close or far we consider something to be from our here and now. The premise is that if we think something is psychologically close, we are more likely to act and create change because we are more concerned, more connected; whereas if we think something is distant, we might assume that the thing is less likely to happen to or affect us and thus we are less likely to act.

Psychological distance has four dimensions, temporal (now, the past or the future), spatial distance (near or far), social distance (a friend or a stranger), and hypotheticality (what could be or might have been).[18] Thus psychological distance refers to whom an event occurs, where it occurs, when it occurs and how likely it is to happen. Building on this, our actions regarding an issue are informed by our perceived proximity, whether it will impact us, when it will impact us and/or whether we have a responsibility to act.[19] As such, reducing psychological distance through having an issue happen to the individual, now, is key to

Human Resources

- Human Resources is common parlance in businesses. However, it is a metaphor that reinforces thinking of humans as being little more than component parts that should be used up and managed as another unit of production would be. Consequently, alternative terms might be useful such as people, colleagues and wellbeing. In turn this might shift the conversation in a business from being resource efficient to considering what would be needed to make the business optimised for human wellbeing.

Machine and Organism

- The challenge of these metaphors is that they perpetuate the notion that the business is separate to the humans that constitute it. Further, it implies a mode of thinking that the business needs to continue in opposition to society and our surroundings. It is not our businesses that need to thrive, but our societies and businesses that enable that will be more fluid in their thinking and in turn more innovative.

Five Forces

- The five forces visual metaphor is one where the business in the centre and the forces impacting it are acting on this central business. Four of the forces are the bargaining power of suppliers, of buyers, the threat of new entrants and substitute products and services. The fifth force is the industry rivalry, the central business is facing. While the systemic nature of the model is useful for strategic planning, its visual metaphor can arguably reinforce a mentality that a business is under siege, such a situation is not ideal for a businesses' productivity.

Figure 8.1 Considering some metaphors

prompting them to act. In turn, this implies that the psychological distance we ascribe to something is impacted by the language we use.

One of the challenges is that business language can tend to the abstract and objective. This contributes to a reduced sense of an individual's connection to issues. Hence, collapsing psychological distance through changing language could encourage action, particularly action that improves outcomes for all. Outlined in Figure 8.2 are the results from a global study that asked respondents to consider different challenge questions in matching pairs.[20] One question was phrased in relatively standard business language, the other in a manner that collapsed psychological distance.

As can be seen in Figure 8.2, phrasing issues in a manner that collapses psychological distance is considered more likely to spur action; the air we breathe, the water we drink, our neighborhood. Thus, phrasing an issue in a manner that makes it about us is more likely to result in us responding with action. This indicates that it may be possible to enhance your business's ability to act meaningfully in our surroundings and purposefully to benefit itself and society through changing the language you use to reduce psychological distance. For example, you might change language from your business addressing atmospheric emissions and pollutants to something simpler, such as asking: Would I want to breathe this? Such phrasing reduces psychological distance and puts you and your leaders at the center of the issue or problem.

To summarize, metaphors and psychological distance matter, metaphors that evoke images of war, or describe the business as a machine or an organism are not enabling of outcomes that are conducive to an understanding that a business is embedded. Rather they are conducive to outcomes that are antagonistic and pit us, our society and our surroundings against the abstract, non-graspable entity that is a business. Reducing psychological distance and putting ourselves at the heart of the issue can spur action.

We are often asked by executives and students alike: What metaphors are advisable to be applied to our business? Our response is to consider business as a tool for us to use for us. This answer builds from an understanding that businesses are rarely established as ends in themselves. Rather they arise from the interactions of people and their shared understanding of what they would like to achieve, what problem they would like to solve. As such, businesses are tools of collective action that we use to shape our future; they are not separate to the people that

- In business we deal in abstract terms like the environment or society, yet these conceptual spaces are not separate to us, as you read this you are breathing air, you are a component of society, you are made of our surroundings.

- The chart highlights the results from a global survey of more than 600 business people. They were asked which question in each pair did they believe was more likely to spur action regarding more sustainable outcomes.

- As can be seen the results are relatively conclusive, that phrasing an issue in a manner that puts the individual at the centre of the action and thus reduces psychological distance is considered more likely to spur action.

- Consequently, a business aiming to become Future Normal would consider shifting the way it phrased issues as asking questions that are phrased to collapse psychological distance will likely spur action.

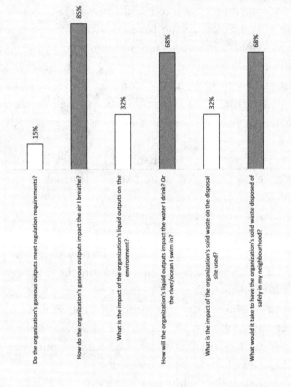

Question	%
Do the organization's gaseous outputs meet regulation requirements?	15%
How do the organization's gaseous outputs impact the air I breathe?	85%
What is the impact of the organization's liquid outputs on the environment?	32%
How will the organization's liquid outputs impact the water I drink? Or the river/ocean I swim in?	68%
What is the impact of the organization's solid waste on the disposal site used?	32%
What would it take to have the organization's solid waste disposed of safely in my neighbourhood?	68%

Figure 8.2 Questions to drive action

Adapted from: Barter, N., & Alston-Knox, C. (2021). Sustainable outcomes: INS/IEO and the relevance of proximity and control to drive change. *Sustainability Accounting, Management and Policy Journal, 12*(1), 105–129. https://doi.org/10.1108/SAMPJ-10-2018-0275.

constitute them. Hence a business is not an end in itself, and our preferred way to describe them is as a tool to enable outcomes for all.

APPLYING THE QUESTION

The challenge question at the core of this chapter regarding whether your business uses language that enables is a question that is focused on ensuring your business uses metaphors that do not perpetuate dehumanization or the prioritization of business relative to society and our surroundings and uses phraseology that decreases psychological distance to galvanize it to action. At a high level, this is relatively easily conceptualized and understood. However, distilling this change through a business and its stakeholders is a process that should proceed slowly, purposeful incrementalism is key. This is because conversations about language can be challenging.

The first step is to have a conversation with a small group of colleagues from a range of your business functions. This conversation should aim to discuss the metaphors the business uses in different aspects of its operations, relationships with stakeholders and so forth. Prompts to drive this conversation include, but are not limited to: What are the current metaphors used? What do these enable? What do they hide? What do they say about us as a business? An example that can aid this exploration is to consider not just the metaphors discussed, but also others such as the term 'consumers' which is commonly used to describe customers. This term can be seen as objectionable as it likens human customers to bovine grazers.[21] Admittedly such a comparison may or may not chime with you and your business. However, what is clear is that the term 'consumers' singularly fails to consider your customers as whole human beings.

Turning to the war-like metaphors that your business probably uses, perhaps ask: Who or what is the business at war with? Why? Does it have to be that way? What if it used co-operative language rather than the language of war? Admittedly as you read this, you may be imagining the challenge of the conversation and colleagues' cynicism. This is to be expected; hence the approach is purposeful incrementalism with curiosity.

Having begun the exploration around metaphors, conducted initial conversations and worked out next steps, the starting point for an exploration of psychological distance is the same; have an initial conversation with a small group of colleagues. In this conversation the focus is the language your business uses to describe the issues it faces and its impacts on society and our surroundings. For example, your business might use the term 'environment'. Why? Where is the environment? Our experience of pondering this question with executives and students always lands them in the same place: They are it, it is everywhere and hence the term is not particularly useful. Building on this, other points of investigation include: Does your business ever consider the air we breathe or the water we drink? Or does it use more distant language, such as 'atmosphere'? Why? When you explore this line of thinking it is likely you will realize that few businesses have ever made the air we breathe cleaner through their operations. Could your business be one of the few? Moving from these material considerations, other questions that collapse psychological distance and reinforce generational thinking include: Which parts of your business operation would you be happy for your children to work in? Which parts would you not want them to work in? Is it okay for your business to have employees working in settings or roles that you would be uncomfortable with your children working in? Alternatively, which suppliers would you be happy for your children to work for, in which countries and in which roles? And which not? If the answers to such questions are mostly negative, then your business is facing a clear challenge that is hindering it from becoming Future Normal and a business that your children will be proud of.

Having conducted these initial conversations, a series of exploratory workshops with colleagues is a good next step. These workshops will not only flush out new thinking as new metaphors and challenge questions are outlined, they will also allow you to understand if the confidence to make a change to your business can emerge and under what conditions.

To close, exploring whether your business has the right language to become Future Normal will challenge conventions. However, if you understand your business as a tool to be used by us for us, such exploration is required, especially because the way we talk has everything to do with the way we act.[22] Businesses that avoid dehumanizing metaphors and instead use ones that collapse psychological distance are those that will create change and be evermore able to act meaningfully and purposefully in our surroundings to benefit itself and society.

NOTES

1 See for example: Ferraro, F., Pfeffer, J., & Sutton, R.I. (2005). Economics language and assumptions: How theories can become self-fulfilling. *Academy of Management*

Review, 30(1), 8-24. https://doi.org/10.5465/amr.2005.15281412. In this article, the authors describe how dominant assumptions, language, and ideas can influence behavior, including behavior in organizations, concluding that "…theories become dominant when their language is widely and mindlessly used and their assumptions become accepted and normatively valued, regardless of their empirical validity" (p.21).

2 For further discussion of everyday metaphors, beyond those you might identify through your own reflections, see Gareth Morgan's 1986 book *Images of Organization*. In this book, Morgan introduces the use of metaphors to understand organizations and solve organizational problems, in so doing demonstrating how metaphors are central to our thinking about organizations and management. A more recent article where Morgan reflects on his book twenty-five years later may also be of interest. See: Morgan, G. (2011). Reflections on *Images of Organization* and its implications for organization and environment. *Organization & Environment*, 24(4), 459-478. https://doi.org/10.1177/1086026611434274. Alternatively, you might like to read Suzanne Romaine's article that examines the role of metaphors in discourse on key environmental issues: Romaine, S. (1996). War and peace in the global greenhouse: Metaphors we die by. *Metaphor and Symbol*, 11(3), 175-194. https://doi.org/10.1207/s15327868ms1103_1.

3 Nick examines the dominance of machine and organism metaphors in organizational studies in more detail in a 2013 article written with Sally Russell. See: Barter, N., & Russell, S. (2013). Organizational metaphors and sustainable development: Enabling or inhibiting? *Sustainability Accounting, Management and Policy Journal*, 4(2), 145-162. https://doi.org/10.1108/SAMPJ-Jan-2012-0002.

4 A full description of the study is published as: Liberman, V., Samuels, S.M., & Ross, L. (2004). The name of the game: Predictive power of reputations versus situational labels in determining prisoner's dilemma game moves. *Personality and Social Psychology Bulletin*, 30(9), 1175-1185. https://doi.org/10.1177/0146167204264004.

5 Most introductory microeconomics textbooks provide a detailed explanation of the prisoner's dilemma. See for example, chapter 17 of Mankiw, N. (2020). *Principles of Microeconomics* (9th ed.). Cengage Learning, USA.

6 Nick explores this in more detail in a 2020 article written with Clair Alston-Knox. See: Barter, N., & Alston-Knox, C. (2021). Sustainable outcomes: INS/IEO and the relevance of proximity and control to drive change. *Sustainability Accounting, Management and Policy Journal*, 12(1), 105-129. https://doi.org/10.1108/SAMPJ-10-2018-0275.

7 In their 2014 article published in the *International Journal of Psychology*, Robert Gifford and Andreas Nilsson review personal and social influences on pro-environmental concern and behavior, including the role of proximity. See: Gifford, R., & Nilsson, A. (2014). Personal and social factors that influence pro-environmental concern and behaviour: A review. *International Journal of Psychology*, 49(3), 141-157. https://doi.org/10.1002/ijop.12034.

8 Again see: Barter, N., & Russell, S. (2013). Organisational metaphors and sustainable development: Enabling or inhibiting? *Sustainability Accounting, Management and Policy Journal*, 4(2), 145-162. https://doi.org/10.1108/SAMPJ-Jan-2012-0002.

9 See Endnote 2 above.

10 In his 1991 article published in the *Academy of Management Review*, organization and leadership theorist Haridimos Tsoukas expands this discussion and proposes a methodology for the development of metaphors to yield deeper organizational scientific knowledge. See: Tsoukas, H. (1991). The missing link: A transformational view of metaphors in organizational science. *Academy of Management Review*, 16(3), 566-585. https://doi.org/10.5465/amr.1991.4279478.

11 For further discussion about this metaphor and many others, see George Lakoff and Mark Turner's 2009 book *More Than Cool Reason: A Field Guide to Poetic Metaphor*. The University of Chicago Press.

12 Stepping back and taking the time to reflect that such a book is used to support the teaching of business strategy is sobering.

13 See the following article for a more complete list: Audebrand, L.K. (2010). Sustainability in strategic management education: The quest for new root metaphors. *Academy of Management Learning & Education*, 9(3), 413-428. https://doi.org/10.5465/amle.9.3.zqr413.

14 As an example of this type of thinking, in 1999, Andy Grove, ex CEO of Intel, published a book *Only the Paranoid Survive: How to Exploit the Crisis Points that Challenge Every Company*. We argue that while individuals in any organization should be aware of alternative solutions offered by other companies, this heightened state of awareness should not be framed within a war context that could tip into paranoia. Rather, be aware, but don't be anxious, be helpful. This is explored further in Chapter 11. The premise for our argument is that we achieve more through enabling others than we do coming from a position of fear or paranoia.

15 For further discussion, consider the following article: Gibbon, J. (2012). Understandings of accountability: An autoethnographic account using metaphor. *Critical Perspectives on Accounting*, 23(3), 201-212. https://doi.org/10.1016/j.cpa.2011.12.005.

16 For example, as noted in Chapter 2 (Endnote 1), ExxonMobil knew about and sought to suppress climate science to continue to pursue profits from fossil fuel extraction and sale.

17 See Chapter 2.

18 For a more complete discussion of psychological distance, see: Liberman, N., Trope, Y., & Stephan, E. (2007). Psychological distance. In A.W. Kruglanski & E.T. Higgins (Eds.), *Social Psychology: Handbook of Basic Principles* (pp. 353–381). The Guilford Press.

19 While significant, psychological distance is not the only barrier to action. For example, Robert Gifford identifies 30 specific manifestations stemming from seven general psychological barriers in his review of psychological barriers to climate action. See: Gifford, R. (2011). The dragons of inaction: Psychological barriers that limit climate change mitigation and adaptation. *American Psychologist*, 66(4), 290-302. https://doi.org/10.1037/a0023566.

20 A full description of this study can be found in: Barter, N., & Alston-Knox, C. (2021). Sustainable outcomes: INS/IEO and the relevance of proximity and control to drive change. *Sustainability Accounting, Management and Policy Journal*, 12(1), 105-129. https://doi.org/10.1108/SAMPJ-10-2018-0275.

21 This comparison was made by the CEO of a company interviewed as part of Nick's Ph.D. and is discussed in: Barter, N., & Russell, S. (2013). Organisational metaphors and sustainable development: Enabling or inhibiting? *Sustainability Accounting, Management and Policy Journal*, 4(2), 145-162. https://doi.org/10.1108/SAMPJ-Jan-2012-0002.

22 For example, there is evidence to suggest that businesses that talk long-term tend to develop long-term stakeholder relationships and deliver long-term returns. See: Eccles, R.G., Ioannou, I., & Serafeim, G. (2014). The impact of corporate sustainability on organizational processes and performance. *Management Science*, 60(11), 2835-2857. https://doi.org/10.1287/mnsc.2014.1984.

Nine

At some time in our lives, we have all pressed our bare foot into the sand on a beach or our booted foot into the mud on a path, leaving a footprint. We may even have trod carefully to avoid causing unnecessary damage. Hence, we all understand that how hard we press dictates the depth of the imprint and the harm that might be done. This understanding also applies to businesses as they become ever more attuned to their footprint, particularly as it relates to carbon. The challenge inherent to the question of this chapter – does your business understand its footprint and tread carefully – is, therefore, intuitively understood. There is little theory to tackle, as on our materially closed planet[1] it is relatively easy to appreciate that a business changes our surroundings through its sourcing of inputs and production of outputs. There is no free lunch, everything we produce has a cost, whether we ascribe a monetary value to it or not. For example, the chair you are sitting on, or the desk you are sitting at, everything around you, comes from our planet and the raw materials would have at some time been part of a functioning ecosystem. Everything has a footprint; the question is how deep it is and could we have trod more lightly?

This chapter introduces the concept of an ecological footprint, before narrowing the focus to carbon, as carbon footprints are an obvious entry point.[2] This does not negate that it is possible to calculate other footprints,[3] it simply recognizes that carbon is likely your most pressing concern. Whatever the footprint being calculated, the principles remain the same. An even more challenging question is then posed: What is the right size for your business? That is, the deeper challenge behind the question framing this chapter is whether your business's footprint is

100

DOI: 10.4324/9781003360636-11

appropriate, does it make sense, does your business tread carefully enough in the context of a single planet? The chapter then brings forward a case study, the Artwork Ingredient List, before outlining a process for application.

FRAMING

All businesses produce financial reports, statements of financial data showing what they have received and spent in any given period. Such statements matter to the financial health of a business, yet they tell us next to nothing about the footprint of the business, how hard it is treading on society and our surroundings to produce its financial outcomes. This lack of insight can often be exacerbated because financial statements are limited to that which has a monetary price. Yet the footprint of a business spreads beyond dollars and cents.[4] Consequently, and as discussed in Chapter 7, financial statements are a partial view, a view that can be likened to seeing a business as if it floats on clouds free of material concerns. Thus, the partiality of the numbers can trap individuals into a numerical logic, where the only concern is how the numbers rise or fall and the implications of such movements are lost. Yet behind numbers are behaviors and physical impacts. Hence there is a need to widen the aperture to more than money in order to understand the footprint of the business and whether it is treading carefully.

The broadest conceptualization of a footprint is an ecological footprint.[5] First introduced by Mathis Wackernagel and William E. Rees,[6] as defined by the Global Footprint Network, an ecological footprint measures how much nature we have and how much nature we use. If our demand for nature outstrips our supply, we have what is termed a biocapacity deficit; if the situation is reversed, we have a biocapacity reserve.[7] Current estimates suggest that as a planet we are in deficit, needing 1.75 Earths to maintain our lifestyles, and we need to go back as far as 1970 to be at a time when demand and supply were balanced. Each year we fill this deficit by drawing down stocks and accumulating wastes.[8]

Moving from the wide perspective of the Earth, footprint calculations have been conducted on individual countries. These calculations reveal some interesting results, as shown in Figure 9.1. The average American has an ecological footprint of 8.1 global hectares (gha)[9] relative to a per capita biocapacity of 3.4gha. Thus, on average, everyone in America is in deficit by 4.7gha. The Earth has an average per capita biocapacity of

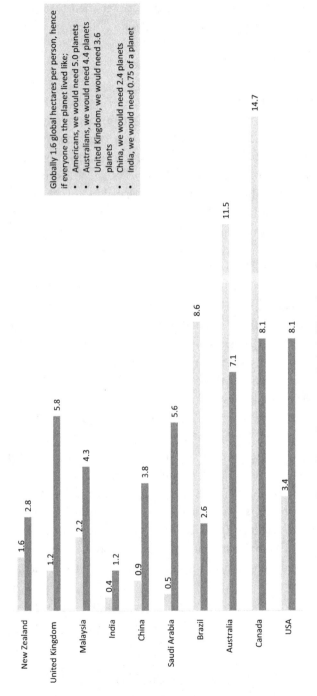

Globally 1.6 global hectares per person, hence if everyone on the planet lived like;
- Americans, we would need 5.0 planets
- Australians, we would need 4.4 planets
- United Kingdom, we would need 3.6 planets
- China, we would need 2.4 planets
- India, we would need 0.75 of a planet

Biocapacity per Person   ▮ Ecological Footprint per Person

Figure 9.1 Ecological footprint for select countries

The data for these figures is from the following website, accessed on the 31 January 2022 and is according to the website 2018 data – Open Data Platform (footprintnetwork.org).

1.6gha. Thus, if all of us lived like Americans, we would need more than five Earths. The situation is not dissimilar for Australians, Canadians and the British, who all have a heavy footprint per person. Narrowing the perspective further, the question that emerges is the footprint of individual businesses and whether they operate as if there is one Earth.

Climate change is a current and pervasive challenge. If left unchecked, climate change will lead to sea level rises, species extinction, biodiversity loss, floods and the dislocation of millions of people.[10] The effects are already being felt as we experience an increased frequency of what were previously considered 'once in a century' weather events.[11] To counter the challenge of climate change, humanity has broadly committed to the Paris Agreement, a legally binding international treaty adopted by 196 nations at the UN Climate Change Conference in Paris, France in 2015. The Paris Agreement has an overarching goal to limit the increase in global average temperature to well below 2°C above pre-industrial levels and to pursue efforts to limit the increase to 1.5°C.[12] However, as evidence mounts on the risks associated with crossing the 1.5°C threshold, the global community has become focused on the need to limit warming to 1.5°C. To achieve this, greenhouse gas emissions need to be reduced by 45 percent by 2030 and reach net zero by 2050.[13]

Businesses must play a role in reaching net zero. The Science Based Targets initiative[14] drives ambitious climate action in the private sector by enabling organizations to set science-based emissions reduction targets. As of April 2023, over 4,800 companies had joined the initiative, of which almost 2,500 had approved and independently validated emissions reduction targets. Despite this progress and an acknowledgement of the risks associated with failure, there is discussion about whether limiting warming to 1.5°C is achievable, given we have already experienced 1.1°C of warming as of 2023, and at current rates of emissions the window for action is rapidly closing.[15]

For a business, the first step in reducing its carbon footprint is to know what it currently is: the baseline. A baseline is relatively simple to establish; several consultancies provide carbon audits. In addition to knowing the volume of emissions, an audit will allow your business to understand how its emissions vary across emission scopes 1, 2 and 3,[16] thus allowing a plan for reduction to be made, ideally in alignment with the Paris Agreement. As shown in Figure 9.2, this plan could explore opportunities for the business to be a net sink for greenhouse gas emissions, taking emissions out of the atmosphere – that is, going beyond net zero.

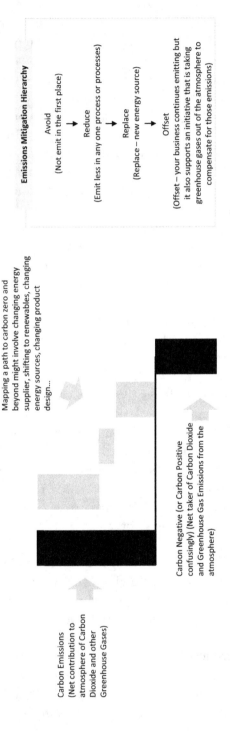

Figure 9.2 Schematic on carbon footprint and emissions mitigation hierarchy

The emissions mitigation hierarchy is adapted from the following website – https://sustainable.columbia.edu/content/greenhouse-gas-mitigation-hierarchy.

Figure 9.2 also illustrates a hierarchy of strategies that should be considered for lowering emissions. The first is to *avoid* making emissions in the first place, the second to *reduce* the volume of emissions, the third to *replace* the process so that, for example, it is powered by a non-emitting energy source. Only after the first three strategies have been employed should the fourth strategy, *offsetting*, be considered. This is partly because the offset market is not yet fully developed and the effectiveness of offsets is subject to considerable uncertainty,[17] but also because relying on offsets delays your investment in innovations that will reduce emissions and make your business fit for the coming decades. Note also that putting faith in carbon capture and storage is misplaced, as the technology remains untested at scale. In 2021 carbon capture and storage captured just 0.1 percent of global emissions, with the International Energy Agency predicting this to increase to a still insignificant 0.5 percent by 2030.[18]

Having considered the business and its carbon footprint, another challenge that emerges is the more philosophical question regarding the optimal size of the business. For many businesses, particularly those listed on stock exchanges, the unwritten rule is that a business must grow, there is no limit. The need to grow is unquestioned, yet unending growth without purpose makes little sense in the context of a single planet. While questioning the size of a business will not yield a single static answer, as optimal size is dynamic, depending on an everchanging context. To frame your thinking, consider the microeconomic concepts of marginal cost and marginal benefit. The former is the cost associated with an incremental (marginal) change, the latter the benefit of that change. The application of these concepts is typically to production, wherein the marginal cost is the cost associated with producing one more unit of a good or service; the marginal benefit, the benefit from doing so. The theory is that at some point marginal costs will increase as production increases, whereas marginal benefits will decline. Then, as shown in Figure 9.3, there is a crossover point depicting the optimal level of production. Typically, this theory only considers that which has a financial price, however when considering the size of your business you should consider more than money. For example, reflect on the marginal benefit of an increase in your footprint relative to the marginal cost of that increase. From here you can start to ponder the optimal size for your business.

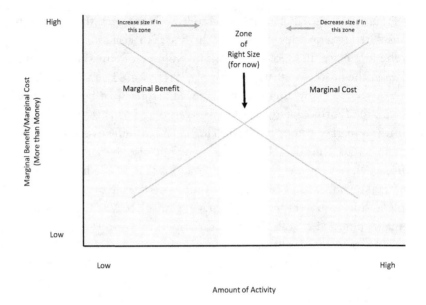

High

Increase size if in this zone →

Zone
of
Right Size
(for now)
↓

Decrease size if in this zone ←

Marginal Benefit/Marginal Cost (More than Money)

Marginal Benefit

Marginal Cost

Low

Low

High

Amount of Activity

Figure 9.3 Schematic on right sizing your business

Having considered some of the key concepts regarding the footprint of your business and how it might be reduced, the following section offers further discussion on applying these concepts, starting with an example, the Artwork Ingredient List.

APPLYING THE QUESTION

Understanding its footprint and treading more carefully is a key consideration for Urban Art Projects (UAP), one of the world's largest art manufacturers.[19] In advising them on how to begin to understand their footprint, the concept of an ingredient list was brought forward. An ingredient list is something we are all familiar with. Such lists provide an element of transparency that can enable us to make more informed decisions about our purchases.[20] Ingredient lists, however, can also hide much, for example the label on your shirt may tell you that it is made of cotton, but it says little about where the cotton came from, the working conditions of those who produced the cotton or the shirt, the amount of energy used and waste produced, or the greenhouse gas emissions associated with production and transport.

These gaps in transparency informed the development of UAP's Artwork Ingredient List, a tool that calculates an artwork's carbon emissions.[21] While the development of the tool was not straightforward, the starting point was to better understand UAP's production processes. This involved understanding key suppliers, UAP's foundry, their pattern making, their paint workshop, their outbound logistics and so on, essentially reviewing their whole value chain. Once this process was understood, a case study was investigated, allowing a refined level of detail to come forward, such as: Which materials were in the artwork, who in particular supplied those materials, the distance they travelled to the manufacturing site, how they were transported, how much material was in the final product, how much was waste, what happened to the waste, how the materials were tooled in manufacture, what tools were used and for how long, how the final art was packaged, where the final art was transported to, and whether the final artwork used energy in its display and if so, how much and of what type. All these inputs were captured and brought together in a database, with emissions factors[22] and calculations certified by UK consultancy Carbon Footprint[23].

Taken together, these data allowed the greenhouse gas emissions for the artwork across scopes 1, 2 and 3 to be calculated. Importantly, not only did the tool reveal greenhouse gas emissions associated with the artwork, it also provided UAP transparency on waste, time spent on production and tools used. Consequently, from a desire to improve its understanding of its carbon footprint and tread more carefully, the conceptual catalyst of an ingredient list enabled UAP to develop a tool that provides insights into its operations against a range of parameters, including time, tools, energy, materials, distance, transport type, emissions and waste. Further, UAP are now better able to provide pre-production guidance to clients on reducing footprints, and thus the tool has both predictive and summative capabilities.

While the Artwork Ingredient List has helped UAP consider its footprint, such an approach may not be right for every business. Nonetheless, the principle behind the tool holds; developing a carbon footprint baseline is the first key task. From there a plan to reduce emissions can be developed, remaining cognizant of the hierarchy of actions highlighted in Figure 9.2. In developing this plan, it is important to talk to stakeholders, especially suppliers. Not only because they share this challenge, as reducing emissions should be on everyone's agenda, but also because they are likely to be able to help. For example, calling your energy provider will unleash a wave of help from them, as they will want to keep you as a customer. If this is not the case, it may be time to find a new energy provider. Consequently, a basic frame of audit, discussion with stakeholders and plan implementation is the way forward, and this frame applies to all your footprints. Following carbon, our recommendation would be water and then biodiversity.

Moving beyond the various footprints of your business, this chapter also raised the challenge of considering the right size for your business. This is a fundamental question that is at the core of treading carefully. To explore this question, start with a small group of trusted colleagues. During this session explore additional questions such as: Why are we growing? What are we hoping to achieve via this growth? What are the positives and negatives of growth? As an aside, when working with organizations it frequently astounds us that very few managers can articulate why growth is necessary, beyond the fact that it is built into their key performance indicators and 'something you do'. In discussing these questions, you and your colleagues might discuss numbers and targets. This is appropriate, but go deeper and ask why these numbers? This type of exploration is philosophical, and it will cut to the core of your business and what it is trying to achieve. In this way it will take you back to the territory of the first challenge question in the Future Normal framework: Does the vision of your business perpetuate a world you want to live in? There is no perfect answer regarding the right size of your business, so do not be afraid of a fuzzy, non-specific answer. Nevertheless, the exploration will reveal new insights, even though they may be confronting, as growth is so often considered a natural law of business and strategy.

In closing, your business has a footprint that can be viewed through many lenses, including carbon, water, biodiversity, ecological and social. Understanding the footprint of your business and treading carefully will enable it to act meaningfully in our surroundings and purposefully to benefit society. Also, in understanding its footprint your business should consider its size, even if no easy answer emerges. While understanding your business footprint and asking how it treads can seem like a financial cost, it is a gateway to innovation and quick cost savings as efficiencies in materials and processes are often identified. Building on this and pointing to the next challenge question, one key driver of innovation is where your business seeks inspiration. Does your business learn from nature?

NOTES

1 See Chapter 2 for further discussion.

2 Note that the term 'carbon footprint' is a misnomer, in that all anthropogenic greenhouse gas emissions are captured in the calculation of the footprint, not just carbon dioxide. For example, a carbon footprint may include methane and nitrous oxide emissions. This leads to the concept of global warming potential, a measure of how much energy the emission of one ton of a gas will absorb over a given period, usually 100 years, relative to the emissions of one ton of carbon dioxide. Methane is estimated to have 28 times and nitrous oxide 265 times the warming potential of carbon dioxide. The Greenhouse Gas Protocol provides standards and guidance on calculating emissions, including guidance on the global warming potential of all greenhouse gases. See: https://ghgprotocol.org/.

3 For example, water footprints. The Water Footprint Network offers water footprint assessments for businesses as well as an online tool for calculating personal water footprints. See: https://www.waterfootprint.org/.

4 Notwithstanding the work being undertaken by economists to place monetary values on goods or services without easily observable market prices. Known as 'non-market valuation', the method and practise of placing monetary values on environmental goods and services for which a conventional market price is otherwise unobservable is one of the most fertile areas of research in the field of natural resource and environmental economics. It is also a major area of research in health economics. An introduction to non-market valuation techniques is provided by: Champ, P., Boyle, K., & Brown, T. (eds.) (2017). *A Primer on Nonmarket Valuation* (2nd edition), Springer, Dordrecht.

5 The Global Footprint Network provides a comprehensive overview of ecological footprints, including an online footprint calculator and case studies. See: https://www.footprintnetwork.org/.

6 The ecological footprint was created as part of Wackernagel's Ph.D. research at the University of British Columbia, Canada. Rees was Wackernagel's Ph.D. supervisor.

7 See the Global Footprint Network for further discussion.

8 An alternative way of thinking about the Earth's biocapacity is Earth Overshoot Day, the date when our demand for ecological resources and services exceeds what the Earth can regenerate in that year. In 2022 that date was July 28. See: https://www.overshootday.org/. Take a moment to reflect on this. How would your board or management team react if you told them that this year the business was going to use all its resources by July 28; thereafter drawing down savings or accumulating debt, and that this was going to happen year after year?

9 A global hectare is a biologically productive hectare with world average biological productivity for a given year. See the Global Footprint Network for further discussion.

10 As noted in Chapter 3 (Endnote 3), there is no shortage of scientific and popular literature outlining the potential impacts of climate change on humanity and our surroundings. The definitive source of scientific literature is the IPCC. The IPCC have recently released their Sixth Assessment Report. See: https://www.ipcc.ch/assessment-report/ar6/.

11 As noted in the *Summary for Policymakers Headline Statements* of the second part (Working Group II) of the Sixth Assessment Report, 'Human-induced climate change, including more frequent and intense extreme events, has caused widespread adverse impacts and related losses and damages to nature and people, beyond natural climate variability.' See: https://www.ipcc.ch/report/ar6/wg2/resources/spm-headline-statements/.

12 See: https://unfccc.int/process-and-meetings/the-paris-agreement.

13 See: https://www.un.org/en/climatechange/net-zero-coalition.

14 The Science Based Targets initiative is a partnership between CDP (formerly the Carbon Disclosure Project), the United Nations Global Compact, the World Resources Institute and the World Wide Fund for Nature. Their website includes a searchable dashboard, updated every Thursday, showing companies and financial institutions that have set science-based targets, or have committed to developing targets. See: https://sciencebasedtargets.org/.

15 See for example an article written by E&E News reporter Chelsea Harvey published in *Scientific American*. This article outlines some of the debate about whether the current emissions target is achievable, arguing that it is not, but that there is no political capacity to admit this yet. The article also notes that, whatever the target, emissions reduction will need to continue because of the disastrous impact of higher temperatures. The article can be found here: https://www.scientificamerican.com/article/the-world-will-likely-miss-1-5-degrees-c-why-isnt-anyone-saying-so/.

16 Greenhouse gas accounting and reporting standards define three 'scopes' of emissions. Scope 1 covers direct greenhouse gas emissions, that is emissions from sources that the company owns or controls, such as its vehicles or boilers. Scope 2 covers electricity indirect greenhouse gas emissions, that is greenhouse gas emissions from the generation of electricity the company consumes. Scope 3 covers indirect greenhouse gas emissions, that is emissions not associated with the company itself but those incurred indirectly, such as when buying materials from suppliers or when customers use the company's products. Scopes 1 and 2 are defined to ensure that more than one company will not account for the same emissions in the same scope, that is, to avoid double counting. The Greenhouse Gas Protocol Corporate Accounting and Reporting Standard (revised edition) can be accessed here: https://ghgprotocol.org/corporate-standard.

17 There are a plethora of articles, commentaries, podcasts and documentaries exploring the (in)effectiveness of carbon offset markets. Common concerns include uncertainty around whether the offset project is really taking place; whether emissions are being reduced; whether the reduction in emissions is permanent; whether there is carbon leakage (or the project simply shifts emissions elsewhere); and whether broader environmental issues or the needs of local communities are considered. See as an example, this article from Bloomberg: https://www.bloomberg.com/features/2020-nature-conservancy-carbon-offsets-trees/.

18 All data is sourced from the International Energy Agency (https://www.iea.org/). For specific data on carbon capture and storage, see: https://www.iea.org/fuels-and-technologies/carbon-capture-utilisation-and-storage.

19 UAP is a truly remarkable company. Starting from humble beginnings in Brisbane, Australia, in 1993, UAP has become a leader in public art and architectural design solutions and manufacturing, and collaborates with influential creatives from around the globe. Among many other claims to fame, they are responsible for producing the Oscar statuettes, see: https://edition.cnn.com/interactive/2023/03/entertainm ent/oscar-statuette-design-cnnphotos/. We are very fortunate to have worked with UAP for several years, particularly in helping them with Project One Earth, their commitment to sustainability, systems thinking and eco-efficiency. For more about UAP, see: https://www.uapcompany.com/about. For more about Project One Earth, see: https://www.uapcompany.com/initiatives/one-earth.

20 As an example, labels highlighting the carbon emissions associated with cans of soup have been shown to shift purchase choices away from higher-emission options. See: Camilleri, A.R., Larrick, R.P., Hossain, S., & Patino-Echeverri, D. (2019). Consumers underestimate the emissions associated with food but are aided by labels. *Nature Climate Change*, 9, 53-58. https://doi.org/10.1038/s41558-018-0354-z.

21 For further information about the Artwork Ingredient List, see: https://www.uap company.com/news/artwork-ingredient-list.

22 An emission factor is a coefficient that describes the rate at which a given activity releases greenhouse gases into the atmosphere.

23 See: https://www.carbonfootprint.com/. See the Greenhouse Gas Protocol Corporate Accounting and Reporting Standard (revised edition) for more information (link in Endnote 16 above).

Ten

It is difficult to discuss nature without resorting to some kind of hyperbole or cliché. Nature often defies description, particularly when it instils a sense of awe and wonder. When we do describe it, we often trick ourselves and characterize it as something separate to us, something we are not part of. As previously discussed, this separation is an illusion; we are embedded in, and part of, nature. In business we often describe nature by categorizing it and separating it into parts. We do this to aid our understanding, and categorization of nature is at the core of most strategy texts[1] and recent initiatives such as the Taskforce on Nature-related Financial Disclosures (TNFD).[2] For example, the TNFD discusses nature as existing across the four realms of land, ocean, freshwater and atmosphere.[3] Within each of these realms are assets yielding flows of services that are valuable to humans.[4] An asset might be bees, the service their ability to pollinate, the value improved crop yields. This framing can be useful, but it is not the subject of this chapter. Rather, this chapter is about the lessons we can learn from nature, particularly as a source of innovation for business, as nature's ingenuity is ubiquitous.[5]

Specifically, the aim of this chapter is to bring forward several frameworks and lessons that are drawn from nature and can be applied to your business. In turn, as you consider the question of whether your business learns from nature, the aim is to encourage you to explore new angles of inquiry for your business, new perspectives through which you and your colleagues can view your business so that it can tread more carefully and be more resilient. While you may not have the technical answers to specific points raised by the provocations in this question,

DOI: 10.4324/9781003360636-12

this does not matter. Rather, your challenge is to know the principles and, thus, be able to uncover the opportunities that learning from nature offers.

FRAMING

Conventional business thinking tends to be linear. The logic is to extract resources, transform them through a production system, sell the resulting product, and then, sometime later, the customer will likely dispose of the product. Running alongside this linear logic, anything that is not needed is disposed of through landfill or its corollaries, air fill and water fill. This thinking only makes sense on an unlimited and sparsely populated planet, which is not our current context. An overview of this conventional linear logic is offered in Figure 10.1.

While linearity is familiar, as we hit planetary boundaries we need to innovate. One method of doing this is to close the loop and eliminate waste. Eliminating waste can mean not creating it in the first place or using it for something, thus making it an input rather than an output. This includes taking products back at the end of their useful life to repurpose or put back into the production process. This type of thinking is at the core of natural capitalism, a critique of the traditional linear model of capitalism where resources are extracted from, and wastes deposited into, our surroundings.[6] Natural capitalism has four components: (1) improve the efficiency of the use of natural resources; (2) shift to biologically inspired production; (3) pursue a solutions-based model; and (4) reinvest in nature.[7] Taking each of these in turn, improving the efficiency of natural resource use concerns reducing waste through the redesign of the final product and/or production process. This draws upon an argument that a business needs to radically increase the outputs it gets from a given unit of input. In other words, pursue efficiency measures but look beyond labor savings, look to the use of materials too. The second aspect of the framework, biologically inspired production, concerns eliminating the idea of waste, so it is either reused, redirected as inputs for another process of production, or rendered benign or biodegradable when returned to the land, water or air. The third aspect, the solutions-based model, concerns a shift from thinking about the product per se to focusing on the underlying need that is being served by the product and using this as a starting point from which to develop less impactful solutions. For example, selling cars is just one solution to the underlying need that people have for transport. Likewise,

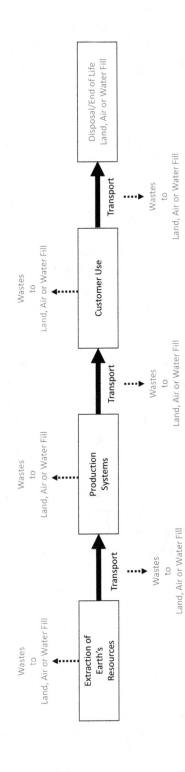

Figure 10.1 Linear thinking

selling lightbulbs is just one solution to the problem of illumination. Offering transport solutions that reduce individual car ownership could reduce the footprint of the car industry. Similarly, illumination can, for example, be provided by light wells that aim to channel daylight. The fourth and final aspect of the natural capitalism framework is reinvesting in nature. This concerns sustaining and restoring our planet's ecosystems and in turn pursuing initiatives that, for example, improve biodiversity and extend forest coverage.

Chiming with natural capitalism is the circular economy initiative promoted by the Ellen MacArthur Foundation.[8] This initiative focuses on how circularity can help businesses eliminate waste and pollution, and through circularity create less demand for extractive industries, leaving more ecosystems intact. A circular economy is based on three principles. The first is to eliminate waste and pollution, the second to circulate products and materials at their highest value and the third to regenerate nature. The circular economy is a popular concept that is well supported and increasingly being pursued by businesses. For example, IKEA have an aspiration to be circular by 2030.[9] In so doing, they are considering challenges such as designing products for disassembly and reuse, repairing products to extend their life and getting end-of-first-life products back. Such challenges shift how the business considers value, especially as IKEA are exploring opportunities for furniture to be a service rather than something a customer owns.[10] Thus, value becomes a flow rather than a one-time exchange.

Inherent to both natural capitalism and circular economy is the elimination of waste. An additional way to do this is by industrial symbiosis, using the waste from one process as an input into another. Given that many wastes from a business' processes may not be useful to the business itself, the challenge of industrial symbiosis is how to move the waste between businesses, so that one business can use another's waste as an input. An often-cited example of this is the Kalundborg Eco-Industrial Park in Denmark. This park is a coming together of 14 different public and private companies to share resources and minimize waste. Some examples of how waste becomes inputs include surplus steam from the power station going to the refinery, which in turn provides waste gas back to the power station, the waste heat from the power station heats homes and a fish farm, and the sludge from the fish farm is sold as fertilizer.[11] While not all industrial processes are, or can be, co-located, the key is that waste streams from your business processes could be inputs for another business. Further, the pursuit of such initiatives could be the start of forming a new business ecosystem that prioritizes eliminating waste.

Building on eliminating waste and closing loops, an additional lens of possible innovation is to consider natural tendencies relative to industrial tendencies.[12] To help understand this perspective, it is worth considering what we would see around us were we to place ourselves in the middle of a forest relative to the middle of an industrial park. The abundance we'd see in a forest would have been formed through natural processes that use water as its base solvent and sunlight as its primary energy source. Chemical processes would have been largely conducted at ambient pressures and temperatures and any by-products would be inputs for another process, nothing would be wasted. Further, the processes would be self-regulating, wherein a form of balance would be realized that did not require excessive controls or management. In contrast, in the industrial park, we would likely see the products stacked high for transportation. We would see the grime, smell the fumes, see the waste that is not reusable, perhaps feel the high temperature and heat of the furnace, and hear the hiss of high pressure being released. As we wandered, we might see a stream and vow not to step in it because of its visible pollution and then ultimately our freedom to roam might be curtailed because of concerns for our safety. Concerns made real by hazardous waste, high pressures, intense heat, toxic fumes and so forth. Finally, the industrial park's processes would likely require constant vigilance lest its processes get out of control.

Evidently the forest and the industrial park offer very different experiences. By pursuing processes that follow natural tendencies we are offered a frontier for innovation. Such innovation is likely to be more benign to our surroundings and ourselves. Further, as production processes that do not deal in heat, pressure, waste, dirt, fumes and excessive controls cost less to operate, these innovations are built for long-term value and optimal efficiency.

Conceptually adjacent to natural tendencies is the field of biomimicry.[13] This involves being inspired by and learning from the strategies of nature. Successful examples of biomimicry include understanding decomposition and how this can help with the waste produced by the fashion industry,[14] learning from termite mounds to aid the design of buildings that stay cool,[15] learning from coral to create colorful, less toxic fibers,[16] and the design of the front of high-speed trains so they move more aero-dynamically through tunnels.[17]

Figure 10.2 provides an overview of the frameworks discussed above. Taken together, these are all lenses through which a business can be inspired by and learn from nature. Intuitively it makes sense. Eliminating waste is better for us, closing the loop uses less materials, operating with natural tendencies is practical, efficient and effective, and learning from nature allows us to benefit from millions of years of nature adapting to solve challenges.

APPLYING THE QUESTION

In applying this question, it is important to recognize that the more you explore and the deeper you dive, the more likely you are to find technical challenges that you may not be equipped to solve. Given this, it is important to maintain at the forefront of your mind the principles of eliminating waste, closing the loop, circularity, industrial symbiosis, natural tendencies and biomimicry, and to recognize that you can bring in the required technical expertise later.

To start exploring this question, begin with a workshop with trusted colleagues. In this workshop, once you have explained the principles, an initial exercise is to map a product in your business and its current process of production, consumption and disposal. Use the schematic in Figure 10.1 as a guide. In undertaking this exercise, an initial focus should be on waste streams. Ask what happens to waste. Does it decompose or is it extra fill for our land, air and water? The next step is to ask how the loop or loops could be closed and whether waste could be eliminated. In doing this, for each part of the process you should focus on asking whether the waste needs to be produced at all and/or does that part of the process have to happen. Then explore whether changing the production process or using waste as an input for another process could be viable. It is possible that as you explore, the inertia of convention overwhelms. For example, your colleagues might argue for the status quo, perhaps for good reason but also perhaps because they are weighed down with tradition, history haunting their present. If you are met with such a response, press on – innovation is built on challenging convention. A useful exercise is to consider whether (metaphorically or literally) the outflow pipes of your process are downstream of your intake pipes. It is likely that they are. However, what if this was not the case? What if your outflow pipes were upstream of your intake pipes? If

Natural Capitalism

- Improve efficiency of use of resources
- Biologically inspired production
- Eliminate waste (Compostable or input for another process - x-ref Industrial Symbiosis)
- Solutions Based model
  - Need View vs Product View
  - Value Flow
  - Ownership – who owns?
- Reinvesting in nature

Circular Economy

- Eliminate waste
- Circulate products and materials
- Regenerate nature
- Lessen demand on extractive industries

Industrial Symbiosis

- One process's waste is another's inputs

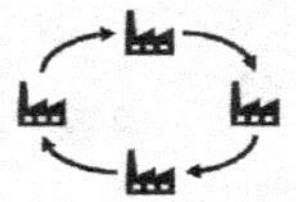

Natural Tendencies vs Industrial Tendencies

Natural Tendencies	vs	Industrial Tendencies
Water as a solvent	vs	Industrial Solvents
Renewable energy	vs	Fossil Fuels
Renewable resources	vs	Non-renewable resources
Ambient temperatures/ pressures	vs	High Temperatures and Pressures
Waste is benign	vs	Waste is hazardous
Self-regulating	vs	Excessive controls
Optimisation for Context	vs	Maximum growth

Biomimicry

- Using nature as an inspiration for new products, services or production methods

Figure 10.2 An overview of frameworks for learning from nature

the clean water intake was downstream of the dirty liquid outflow pipe, or the clean air intake was next to the chimney outlet, it is likely the production methods of your business would be cleaner.[18]

After focusing on closing loops and eliminating waste, the next aspect to explore is natural tendencies and biomimicry. Use each of these concepts as filters through which to consider your processes, products and services. Having done this, the next question to consider is the underlying need the business services. Answering this question might seem simple, yet it is unlikely there will be universal agreement, especially if the conversation shifts away from functional needs to emotional ones. However, having identified the needs, the challenge is to ask what other ways are there to solve these needs and can those methods more closely align with nature? Can they be more benign or less impactful? For example, and as indicated earlier, does the business sell lightbulbs or illumination? Alternatively, does the business sell chairs or the ability to sit? Such questions might seem pedantic, but they will yield insights. Further, such thinking may open new markets. To expand, the consideration of underlying needs has some historical roots within arguments brought forward by Theodore Levitt.[19] He argued that businesses should consider the underlying need they are servicing to avoid a form of myopia by only having a narrow product orientation. As such, he put forward a view that car companies should see themselves in the transport business and oil companies should see themselves in the energy business. Consequently, thinking about underlying needs can be valuable, as it might enable a shift in the business's offerings and an opportunity for it to redefine itself. However, this said, such thinking should be tempered with consideration for what is possible. For example, shifting to selling transport solutions rather than cars could mean moving from a convention of product ownership being transferred to the customer, to ownership being jointly maintained between the business and its customers, and value now operating as a flow as opposed to a single transaction.

When you have completed these initial explorations, it is likely you will have a long list of challenges and potential opportunities for change. This list will need to be prioritized against parameters of impact, investment and time. It is only after this initial prioritization that you will need to enroll different forms of expertise such as engineers, designers and systems thinkers to help develop the detailed business cases for possible investment and implementation.

To close, in exploring the many lenses through which your business can learn from nature, it is likely that it will become more eco-efficient and eco-effective. By eco-efficient we mean doing things well with fewer inputs; by eco-effective we mean doing the right things, things that are compatible with maintaining the Earth's carrying capacity through enhancing eco-systems. Such outcomes will likely reduce costs and complexities – for example, using less inputs reduces supplier costs, producing no waste or pollution reduces discharge fees and potential liabilities. In addition, the opportunities that arise from learning from nature are likely to improve your business returns as your existing customers support such changes with enhanced loyalty while new customers are attracted to your offerings. Thus, learning from nature is likely to have a positive impact on your business. Note, however, that pursuing opportunities is a team sport; to realize any gains your business will need to work with all stakeholders. Hence a consideration will be whether you share what you learn with other companies or not. To not do so is old normal thinking, Future Normal thinking is to share learnings, because this engenders wider systemic change. This approach is the subject of the next chapter and the final question in the Future Normal framework: Does your business lead by enabling others?

NOTES

1 As Nick concludes in a 2016 article published in *Organization & Environment*, strategy texts offer a sclerotic, dehumanized view of the environment that is partitioned into external and internal categories by an organizational boundary. Such a view is not conducive to fostering sustainable outcomes. See: Barter, N. (2016). Strategy textbooks and the environment construct: Are the texts enabling strategists to realize sustainable outcomes? *Organization & Environment*, 29(3), 332-366. https://doi.org/10.1177/10860 26616638130.

2 Taking its inspiration from the Taskforce on Climate-related Financial Disclosures (https://www.fsb-tcfd.org/), the TNFD aims to develop and deliver a risk management and disclosure framework for organizations to report and act on evolving nature-related risks, thus supporting a shift in global financial flows away from nature-negative towards nature-positive outcomes. See: https://tnfd.global/.

3 The TNFD dashboard provides a detailed description of their framework. Within the background material are concepts and definitions, including the TNFD's conceptualization of nature across four realms. See: https://framework.tnfd.global/framework-and-guidance/concepts-and-definitions/definitions-of-nature/.

4 Known as 'ecosystem services', these can be broadly defined as the contributions of nature to human well-being. Ecosystem services are typically classified into provisioning (e.g., plants providing food), regulating (e.g., wetlands purifying water)

or cultural services (e.g., forests for recreation). See further information about the classification of ecosystem services here: https://cices.eu/. In a famous article published in *Nature* in 1997, Robert Costanza and colleagues estimated the annual global total economic value of ecosystem services to be in the range of USD16-54 trillion, with an average of USD33 trillion. At that time, the annual value of the global formal economy was approximately USD18 trillion. See: Costanza, R., d'Arge, R., De Groot, R., Farber, S., Grasso, M., Hannon, B., ... & Van Den Belt, M. (1997). The value of the world's ecosystem services and natural capital. *Nature*, 387, 253-260. https://doi.org/10.1038/387253a0. In 2014 an update was published, estimating the value for 2011 to be USD125 trillion, again approximately double the value of the formal economy at that time. See: Costanza, R., De Groot, R., Sutton, P., Van der Ploeg, S., Anderson, S.J., Kubiszewski, I., ... & Turner, R.K. (2014). Changes in the global value of ecosystem services. *Global Environmental Change*, 26, 152-158. https://doi.org/10.1016/j.gloenvcha.2014.04.002. In developing nations, the gap between the value of ecosystem services and the formal economy is even larger. In a study undertaken on behalf of the Secretariat of the Pacific Regional Environment Programme, Chris and colleagues estimated the total ecosystem service values of the Pacific Island nation of Vanuatu to be almost four times the value of the formal economy. See: Buckwell, A.J., Fleming, C., Smart, J.C., Ware, D., & Mackey, B. (2020). Challenges and sensitivities in assessing total ecosystem service values: Lessons from Vanuatu for the Pacific. *The Journal of Environment & Development*, 29(3), 329-365. https://doi.org/10.1177/10704 96520937033.

5 A very small sample of nature's ingenuity includes whales and other marine species using sonar to navigate, trees communicating and sharing nutrients through the wood wide web, and birds sleeping while in flight. See: Mustill, T. (2022). *How to Speak Whale: A Voyage into the Future of Animal Communication.* Hachette UK; Simard, S. (2021). *Finding the Mother Tree: Uncovering the Wisdom and Intelligence of the Forest.* Penguin UK; and Rattenborg, N.C., Voirin, B., Cruz, S.M., Tisdale, R., Dell'Omo, G., Lipp, H.P., ... & Vyssotski, A.L. (2016). Evidence that birds sleep in mid-flight. *Nature Communications*, 7, 12468. https://doi.org/10.1038/ncomms12468.

6 See: Lovins, A.B., Lovins, L.H., & Hawken, P. (1999). A road map for natural capitalism. *Harvard Business Review*, 77, 145-161.

7 Please note that the actual term is to reinvest in 'natural capital'. However, because the capital metaphor is problematic, particularly as it pertains to our considerations of nature, we have adjusted the language. For a discussion on the problematic nature of the metaphor please refer to Chapter 8 or an article Nick published in 2015: Barter, N. (2015). Natural capital: Dollars and cents/dollars and sense. *Sustainability Accounting, Management and Policy Journal*, 6(3), 366-373. https://doi.org/10.1108/SAMPJ-02-2014-0011.

8 The Ellen MacArthur Foundation emerged from Ellen MacArthur's experience in 2005 of becoming the fastest solo sailor to circumnavigate the Earth. Seventy-one days alone aboard a seventy-five-foot trimaran led Ellen to question the fragility of the systems underpinning our economies, drawing parallels between her yacht and the Earth; in both cases the inhabitants completely reliant on finite resources extracted, used and then disposed of. For more information about the Foundation and the circular economy concept, see: https://ellenmacarthurfoundation.org/.

9 IKEA's ambition to be circular (and climate positive) by 2030 and the various initiatives they are pursuing to achieve this are discussed here: https://about.ikea.com/en/sustainability/a-world-without-waste.

10 See: https://productasaservice.net/ikea-offers-furniture-as-a-service/.

11 See: https://www.symbiosis.dk/en/.

12 This depiction of natural versus industrial tendencies is adapted from a presentation given in 2002 by Tom Gladwin, Emeritus Professor, School of Environment and Sustainability, University of Michigan.

13 See the Biomimicry Institute for further information: https://biomimicry.org/.

14 See: https://biomimicry.org/thenatureoffashion/.

15 See: https://asknature.org/strategy/mound-facilitates-gas-exchange/#.VB52Ry5dUa0.

16 See: https://asknature.org/strategy/protein-turns-sunlight-into-vivid-color/.

17 That the kingfisher was the inspiration for the nose of Japanese bullet trains is a well-documented illustration of biomimicry. See: https://earthsky.org/earth/sunni-robertson-on-how-a-kingfisher-inspired-a-bullet-train/.

18 This challenge regarding the inlet and outlet pipe and their relative location was part of Donella Meadows' argument in her article on the importance of identifying leverage points in systems. See: Meadows, D. (1997). Places to intervene in a system. *Whole Earth*, 91, 78-84.

19 See: Levitt, T. (1960). Marketing myopia. *Harvard Business Review*, 38, 45-56.

Eleven

The assumed *modus operandi* of business is one of being in competition with, rather than being supportive of others. Operating in this way is advanced by business advisors who are forever creating a sense of urgency and fear. The argument goes that their expertise is needed because business is going through turbulent times, and they have the answers, their expertise will allow you to shore up the businesses' defenses, gain ground on rivals and move from defense to offense, as if running your business was some war-like video game.[1]

This creation of a sense of urgency verges on the absurd. The key to success for any business over the long-term is meaningful relationships with customers and other stakeholders, not defensive and offensive posturing. Nevertheless, the notion that a business is in perpetual competition with others and, therefore, must maintain a heightened state of awareness, a level of paranoia, is at the core of most business strategy. Within this core is the misplaced idea that winning and losing is only measured on the singular axis of money and that it is a zero-sum game, your gains are matched by someone else's losses. At the heart of the problem lies an economic theory that, while convenient, is unsuitable for our current context. The implication of this theory is that the interests of business and society are, by construction, misaligned. For a business to succeed in the long-term it must attain and protect a degree of market power, which it then uses to the detriment of its customers. This framing is a choice – it does not have to be a mental cage through which all business strategy is viewed.

Hence, with this question the intent is to offer an alternative perspective that challenges a convention where money is all that matters,

DOI: 10.4324/9781003360636-13

competitors are threats, the game is zero-sum, and the interests of business and society are misaligned. This alternative is about your business enabling others, so that it can enable wider change and act meaningfully in our surroundings and purposefully to benefit itself and society.

FRAMING

Competition is a primary concept in business strategic thinking. Its roots are found in economics, along with the assumption that pursuing profit maximization is the sole goal of any business. Thus, money is the ultimate end, and everything else is a means to this end. As discussed in Chapter 2, this assumption was advanced by economist Milton Friedman when he argued that the one and only social responsibility of business is to maximize profit.[2] This type of thinking is useful if the intent is to be able to mathematically model businesses and their behavior, a favored activity of economists. It is much easier to construct a model when the primary output is ensuring that revenues are greater than costs by the maximum amount, because this reduces the task to a simple single-objective mathematical optimization. The actual messy complexities of humans and how we make decisions can be ignored; we can be simplified to money maximizers. Such thinking works in terms of modelling but fails the everyday test. Businesses rely on human behaviors for their monetary outcomes, yet we humans do not make decisions solely based on money.

Closely associated with the assumption that businesses seek to maximize profit above all else is the theoretical construct of a perfectly competitive market. In this construct, there are many sellers, each producing a very small fraction of the total market output. Likewise, there are many buyers, who perceive the products of all sellers as being identical. Further, all the buyers and sellers have perfect information about product price and quality. It is costless for businesses to enter or exit the market. Individual businesses have no market power and no ability to choose the price of their product. Rather they are price takers, with the price set by invisible market forces that emerge from buyers and sellers interacting. This is a beautiful theory, with a lot of simplistic assumptions that divorce it from our lived reality, further it is not optimal for society. No industry or market operates in such perfect conditions, and if businesses are unable to set prices, the only lever they have left to maximize profits is to lower costs. In fact, the theory of perfect competition implies that this market structure is optimal *because* costs are minimized. While, at first glance, the pursuit of lower costs seems sensible, further interrogation reveals inherent flaws with such a line of thinking. For example, following this logic suggests a business should aim to employ as few people as possible and pay them as little as possible.[3] Further, the business should find the cheapest source of all inputs, regardless of where or in what conditions they are made. In addition, it should make production as low-cost as possible and use the lowest-cost waste disposal, regardless of any impact on us or our surroundings. Unfortunately, too many businesses deploy such strategies, perhaps boosted by the utterances of Friedman and the comfort of economic theories that rationalize such behavior. However, it is not hard to see that these behaviors lead to far from ideal outcomes.

Despite the obvious flaws, the myth of perfect competition being socially optimal persists and ties into another idea reinforced by economic theory. That is, the idea that competitive markets, if left alone, are the optimal means of allocating resources.[4] This illusion is reinforced by the evergreen popularity of *laissez-faire* capitalism, which argues markets should be left to their own devices with minimal government intervention, and in so doing optimal outcomes will emerge. However, this is only true under an extensive set of conditions, as noted by Don Fullerton and Robert Stavins in their 1998 article published in *Nature*:[5]

> Private markets are only efficient if there are no public goods, no externalities, no monopoly buyers or sellers, no increasing returns to scale, no information problems, no transaction costs, no taxes, no common property and no other 'distortions' between the costs paid by buyers and the benefits received by sellers. (p. 433)

As noted, the challenge of competitive markets from an individual business' perspective is that they are unable to set prices and have limited options to increase profitability. The view that competitors are threats, and market power is the key to making as much money as possible is at the core of Michael Porter's 'five forces', which have dominated strategic business thinking for the past 40 years.[6] The argument that supports this five forces model is that a competitive market is terrible for long-run profitability. Thus, as illustrated in Figure 11.1, to make as much money as possible a business should pursue strategies that ensure less power for suppliers and customers, lessen the threat of new entrants and substitutes, and weaken competitors.

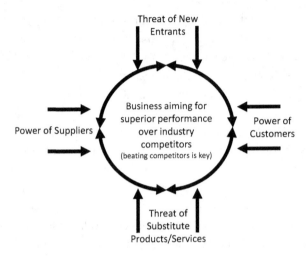

Figure 11.1 Five forces

Image adapted from Porter, M.E., 2008. The five competitive forces that shape strategy. *Harvard Business Review, 86*, p.78.

The logic of such arguments is irrefutable, if illusional base conditions are assumed. Figure 11.2 further illustrates the idea, underpinned by economic theories of market structures and business behavior, that the interests of society and business are misaligned – are, in fact, diametrically opposed. On the right-hand side of the figure, the ideals of perfect competition assume that societal wellbeing is maximized as the market is competitive and governments are helping to maintain this state through, for example, antitrust policies and competition laws. Yet, as highlighted, if a business wants to improve its outcomes it has limited options. It can lower costs with all the flow-on consequences, or attempt to shift market conditions to the left-hand side of Figure 11.2, reducing the number of competitors and increasing market power, thus allowing higher prices to be charged. Thus, Figure 11.2 depicts a model of market structure and business behavior that says societal wellbeing is improved as businesses move to the right of the spectrum, while business profits improve as they move to the left. That is, we have developed and adopted economic theories that at their very core have the desires of society and businesses in conflict. Resting business strategy on economic theories that put businesses in conflict with society makes little sense. Nonetheless, these theories

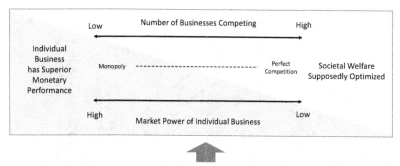

Individual
Business
has Superior
Monetary
Performance

Low · High

Monopoly - Perfect
Competition

Societal Welfare
Supposedly Optimized

High · Low
Market Power of Individual Business

This left to right axis only concerns financial performance and does not consider impacts on society or surroundings unless they are priced. Non-priced items are not even considered.

Figure 11.2 Conventional economic market power spectrum

are encoded within business strategy, Porter's five forces and the ideals of competitive advantage.[7]

As discussed, the thinking that underlies these theories is built on faulty logic. Logic that makes sense for mathematical modelling and possibly for some individuals some of the time, but not for most of us most of the time. Thus, to escape the logic, there is a need to move past notions of winning and losing in a zero-sum game, where money is the only end, competitors are threats, and the interests of business and society are misaligned. Rather, the alternative is to come back to our lived reality and the truth in front of us, wherein business is embedded and not everything that matters has a price. In this shift, depicted in Figure 11.3, we start to understand businesses as something more than money maximizers because they impact us and our surroundings. We start to understand that businesses are tools for humans to produce outcomes, only one of which is money. This type of thinking shifts the logic away from the simple to something more complex, where there is a balance of many measures to be considered, as discussed in Chapter 7.

When shifting to a more realistic perspective, the focus should be on how your business can benefit itself, society and our surroundings. As such, the strategic imperatives change to enabling rather than competing. A primary example of leading for others is the outdoor clothing business, Patagonia. It is a company that takes an approach that differs from the competitive convention; they share

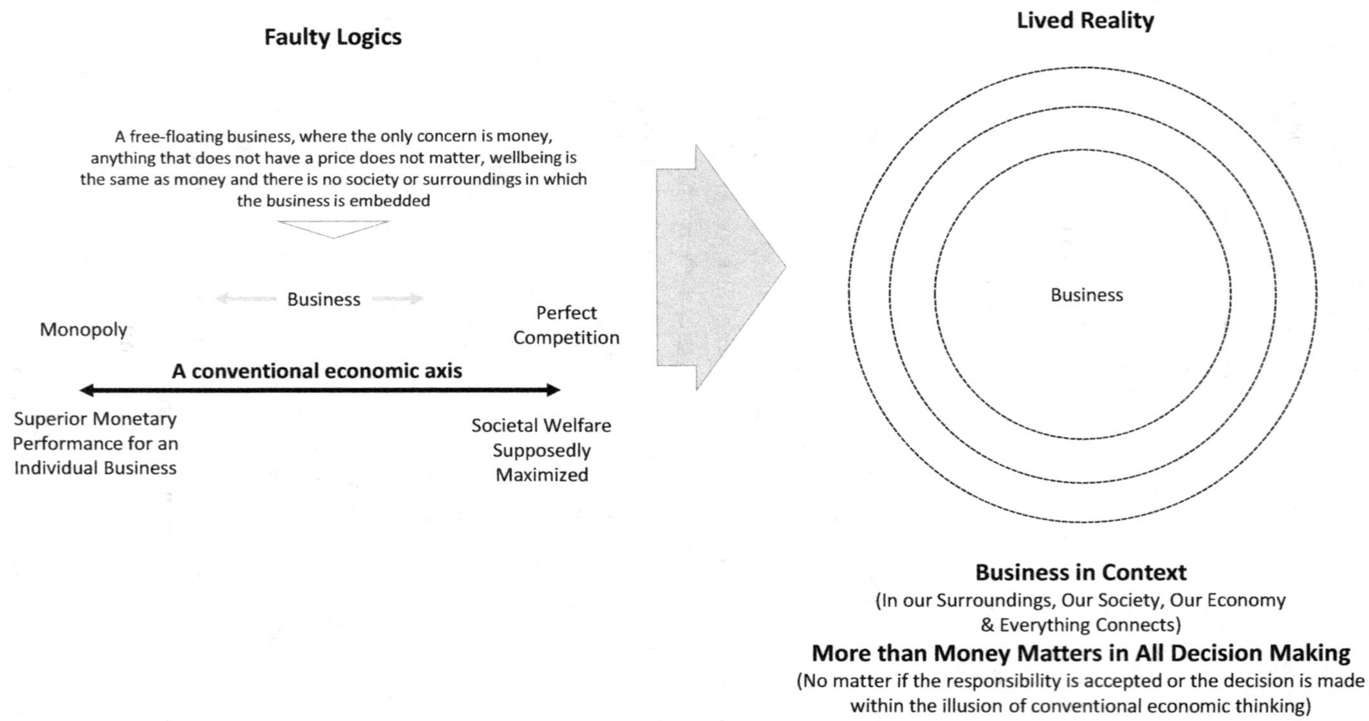

Faulty Logics

A free-floating business, where the only concern is money, anything that does not have a price does not matter, wellbeing is the same as money and there is no society or surroundings in which the business is embedded

Business

A conventional economic axis

Monopoly

Perfect Competition

Superior Monetary Performance for an Individual Business

Societal Welfare Supposedly Maximized

Lived Reality

Business

Business in Context
(In our Surroundings, Our Society, Our Economy & Everything Connects)

More than Money Matters in All Decision Making
(No matter if the responsibility is accepted or the decision is made within the illusion of conventional economic thinking)

Figure 11.3 Shifting from faulty logics to our lived reality

their expertise with Wal-Mart on how to green their supply chain and have advised Nike on using organic cotton.[8] Patagonia are not alone. IKEA, for example, has a strategy that is focused on enabling change in society through pursuing a sustainable business model and sharing what they learn.[9]

Such sharing appears counterintuitive, especially for those stuck in a zero-sum (competitors as threats) conventional mindset. Shifting from convention, however, enables the business to enhance its reputation, and this yields several benefits. For example, it can enhance customer loyalty.[10] Shifting from convention also helps to attract new customers, as surveys indicate that individuals want to buy from businesses that take a stand on issues such as sustainability, transparency and fair employment.[11] Further, talent attraction and employee loyalty improve as individuals are increasingly looking to work for businesses that make a positive difference.[12] Crucially, it also allows those that might conventionally be competitors to improve their outcomes for society and our surroundings at lower cost, as they are learning from the experience of others. Thus, all benefit: Society, surroundings, the lead business, and the conventional competitor.

Finally, as illustrated in Figure 11.4, leading for others can set in motion a virtuous cycle of continuous improvement, as the enhanced performance of the business due to the factors described above gives the business an opportunity to invest over the long-term in further improvements.[13]

APPLYING THE QUESTION

Leading your business in a manner that enables others is a significant shift, particularly if you or your colleagues are caught in a conventional mindset where strategy is the pursuit of market power because money is the only end. The first step in making this shift is to reflect on the companies you consider your business to be in competition with. Do you know the executives, some of the key personnel? When you meet them, do you act like rivals? How many of your colleagues shift from one competitor to the next? Building on this, consider how operating with a competitive mindset has served your business. What have been the positives and negatives for your business, your competitors, those who work with you and your wider stakeholder group? More broadly, how has society benefited? How have our surroundings benefited? Has a conventional, adversarial mindset resulted in a lack of trust in the business?

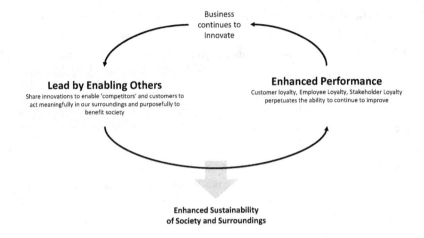

Figure 11.4 Leading by enabling others

Does this show itself in the management culture? The answers to these types of questions are likely to be confronting, and the list of positives and negatives will be substantial. Nevertheless, obvious lessons will emerge about how you would like your business to be. If you struggle with these questions and require additional framing, refer to two figures offered in previous chapters, namely Figure 3.1, 'The shift required' and Figure 5.5, 'The nines framework: Old nine and new nine'.

.Once you have completed this individual reflection, the next step is to start a conversation with some trusted colleagues. This conversation should probably be broken into stages, where you lead them in a group conversation after they have individually reflected on the questions posed above. Additional questions you might like to ask your colleagues both individually and collectively is to name the businesses they truly admire, and why. In support of this line of enquiry, it would be advisable to ask the younger generation which companies they admire. The answer you are likely to receive from the younger generation is that they admire businesses that lead through enabling others as opposed to those that view others as competitive threats. This is because young people want to see businesses that have purpose and wellbeing at their core, take a positive stand on social and environmental challenges, are transparent and listen to stakeholders[14].

Having explored these questions both individually and then within the group, it is important to record what is discussed and note any examples offered about what the business could do to lead by enabling others. In addition to the emerging understanding of what it might mean for your business to lead, you and your colleagues should consider what the implications are for how the business is internally led. Again, record the positives and negatives and the gap between where you are and where you would like to be, and what might need to be done to close that gap. Having done these exercises, the next stage is to widen the conversation to other stakeholders. These conversations will build your understanding of some of the steps that your business could take in the short and long-term.

In making this type of change, you will likely encounter some entrenched cynicism. This means you will need to be in this for the long-term and support the change with visible outcomes. The change to leading by enabling others is a significant step, but it will drive loyalty and the long-term success for your business. Moreover, it will feel better. Building on this, and to reinforce the imperative for this type of change, there is one final consideration. That is, the illusion of economic models that reinforce a perspective that money is all that matters. Alas, none of us live in that world. Given a choice, we tend to buy from businesses that make us feel good. The real value of any business is in its people. However, to avoid the triteness of the last sentence, the value is in the coming together of the business and its stakeholders, particularly customers. What is more, the value of the business is reinforced by whether those stakeholders all keep turning up and supporting the business and buying its products and services. Those stakeholders, all of us, live in a real world of society and surroundings, not a fantasy world of money alone. Hence, why create strategies for your business as if that illusion was real? Rather, if your business acts meaningfully in our surroundings and purposefully to benefit itself and society and achieves this through enabling others it will be a success.

NOTES

1 This language was drawn from an advertisement by management consultants McKinsey & Company, who were promoting a webinar for CEOs on six priorities for turbulent times, replete with imagery of a fencer donning their sabre mask. See: https://www.mckinsey.com/capabilities/strategy-and-corporate-finance/our-insights/what-matters-most-six-priorities-for-ceos-in-turbulent-times.

2 In 1970 Milton Friedman published an article in The New York Times titled 'A Friedman doctrine. The social responsibility of business is to increase profits'. This article

conflates social outcomes with profits and assumes that businesses do not necessarily have an outsized influence on policy development. When Friedman put this forward, the USA was in a cold war with the USSR. Hence, to allude to business being about anything social in its outcomes was a non sequitur. The original article can be found here: https://www.nytimes.com/1970/09/13/archives/a-friedman-doctrine-the-social-responsibility-of-business-is-to.html.

3 For some reason, this logic is rarely applied to executive salaries or bonuses.

4 Taking a moment to defend economic theory. The simplifying assumptions of profit maximization, perfect competition and markets being the most efficient means of allocating resources are all sensible *starting* points for exploring firm behavior, market structures and how to organize economic activity. Deeper interrogation of economic theory unpacks and critiques these assumptions, by for example introducing the myriad of ways markets can fail, the need for equity to be considered alongside efficiency, and for individual behavior to be better understood and modelled, beyond the perfectly rational, self-interested *homo economicus*. Unfortunately, most business graduates and many popular press business commentators have only studied introductory economics and fail to realize, or choose to ignore, that they have only reached the foothills of economic theory. Further exploration would reveal that these theories are, for the most part, abandoned in favor of more realistic descriptions of economic behavior.

5 Fullerton, D., & Stavins, R. (1998). How economists see the environment. *Nature*, 395, 433-434. https://doi.org/10.1038/26606.

6 See: Porter, M.E. (1979). *Harvard Business Review*. How competitive forces shape strategy, 57, 137-145.

7 Competitive advantage is typically discussed within the context of a framework wherein a business has differentiation advantage or cost advantage relative to comparison companies. Thus, it can charge higher prices or produce its outputs more cheaply. Michael Porter's 1985 book *Competitive Advantage: Creating and Sustaining Superior Performance* provides a fuller description.

8 Monte Burke's article in *Forbes Magazine* discusses both the Wal Mart and Nike examples. See: https://www.forbes.com/forbes/2010/0524/rebuilding-sustainability-eco-friendly-mr-green-jeans.html?sh=55033e734299.

9 As mentioned in Chapter 10, IKEA have an aspiration to be circular and climate positive by 2030 and have set strategic goals to achieve this. The fourth goal is to join forces with others and lead by example. See: https://about.ikea.com/en/sustainability/a-world-without-waste.

10 See Frederick Reichheld and Thomas Teal's 1996 book *The Loyalty Effect: The Hidden Force Behind Growth, Profits and Lasting Value* for an in-depth discussion on the impact of customer loyalty.

11 As an example, in their fourteenth annual Global Consumer Pulse Research report, global professional services company Accenture conducted a survey of almost 30,000 people in 35 countries. A key takeaway was that customers aren't just making decisions based on product selection or price, they are assessing what a brand says, what it does and what it stands for. A summary of survey results can be found

Part II: The Challenge Questions

here: https://www.accenture.com/_acnmedia/thought-leadership-assets/pdf/ accenture-competitiveagility-gcpr-pov.pdf. Further, in collaboration with NielsenIQ, McKinsey & Company analyzed five years (2017–2022) of US data to examine sales growth for products that claim to be environmentally and socially responsible. The study concluded there was strong evidence that consumer-expressed sentiments about environmental, social and governance initiatives translate, on average, into actual spending behavior, and that companies don't need to choose between these initiatives and growth, they can achieve both. See: https://www.mckinsey.com/ind ustries/consumer-packaged-goods/our-insights/consumers-care-about-sustainabil ity-and-back-it-up-with-their-wallets.

12 Michelle Mahony's 2022 article in the *Harvard Business Review* outlines five truths of employee value propositions, the first being that the proposition must link to company purpose because people are increasingly looking to join organizations that have a greater purpose beyond profitability. See: https://hbr.org/sponsored/2022/01/ how-to-attract-top-talent-in-2022.

13 A 2014 article published in *Management Science* reports the results of analysis that found high sustainability companies financially outperformed low sustainability companies over the long-term. In so doing, key to the argument is that companies that pursue corporate sustainability have a long-term perspective, which they have fostered through working with all their stakeholders. See: Eccles, R.G., Ioannou, I., & Serafeim, G. (2014). The impact of corporate sustainability on organizational processes and performance. *Management Science*, 60(11), 2835-2857. https://doi.org/ 10.1287/mnsc.2014.1984.

14 These points have been distilled from the World Economic Forum's articles exploring what young people want from businesses. The following two links offer a view of the five things young people want and how the World Economic Forum views young people as key to shaping our future. The message of the articles is that young people want to be involved in dialogue with business leaders and that they want businesses that help to solve the challenges we face in society and our surroundings. In turn, the articles mention that they want businesses to pay their fair share of taxes and be courageous in taking stands on issues. See: https://www.weforum.org/agenda/2023/ 02/youth-workplace-future-davos2023/; and https://www.weforum.org/agenda/ 2021/08/young-people-hold-the-key-to-creating-a-better-future/.

REALIZING THE FUTURE NORMAL
PART III

Twelve

This book is about challenging your business to think afresh about its purpose and its possibilities. It is asking you to shift your business towards becoming one that your children will be proud of, wherein it acts meaningfully in our surroundings and purposefully to benefit itself and society. In so doing, this book has likely made you reconsider the purpose of your business; this is to be expected. There have been debates about the purpose of business throughout history. The current perspective remains caught in the shadow of Milton Friedman's argument from approximately 50 years ago that the only responsibility of a business is to maximize shareholder returns. However, the debate is ongoing; Friedman's utterances dominated for a period, but they are not golden truths. In the 1930s there was debate about whether the purpose of business was shareholder return or to make a broader contribution to the good of society.[1] More recently, it appears that a new compact is emerging even if that compact is not yet fully formed. This book argues that the now radical of a business acting meaningfully in our surroundings and purposefully to benefit itself and society will be the Future Normal, and this shift will deliver long-term value.

To help enable such a shift, we have posed the following eight questions:

1 Does your business's vision perpetuate a world you want to live in?
2 Is your business aligned with our world?
3 Does your business listen to all its stakeholders?
4 Does your business have the metrics?
5 Does your business use language that enables?

DOI: 10.4324/9781003360636-15

6   Does your business understand its footprint and tread carefully?
7   Does your business learn from nature?
8   Does your business lead by enabling others?

These questions are challenging, but questions are not statements or directives – by construction they open conversations. At times these conversations may be confronting, but they are conversations that need to be had and, for many organizations, they are long overdue. Our advice in terms of question order would be to work through them from one to eight. However, if that is not practical, if nothing else, focus on the guiding star that is your business's vision, mission, values and purpose.

The use of questions, and these eight questions in particular, is deliberate. As illustrated in Figure 12.1, in our view, businesses are anchored in two ways. The first is an anchoring to the shared understandings of the people who constitute it, the business participants. The second is that businesses should operate to logics that are informed by our lived reality. Hence to change a business you need to ask those who constitute it different questions, and those questions need to reinforce that businesses are of society and our surroundings.

The Future Normal perspective is one that is moving businesses to accepting the responsibility of operating in a world that is borderless. Thus, where it is commonplace to limit business considerations to money, their acts have never been this limited. Such thinking helps us create theories, build mathematical models and perhaps make knowledge transferable. However, it is too much of a simplification of the world we live in and the decisions we make. Thus, while we may conceptually split our world into different buckets, we must not confuse this simplification with our reality. The Future Normal approach is trying to drag us back to a more complex world, the one we live in. In so doing it is making the basis of our decisions a little harder, as simple quantitative algorithms are not enough. Hence, we now must consider how we run a business through both a quantitative *and* qualitative lens. The development of the qualitative lens is encapsulated by the first question in the framework regarding vision and the associated constructs of purpose, mission and values, and is underpinned by considering our wellbeing as humans. The implications of this question and the seven that follow will emerge from who you and your colleagues have conversations with and the feedback you receive. However, what is certain is that the Future Normal questions will help you shift your business to one that operates

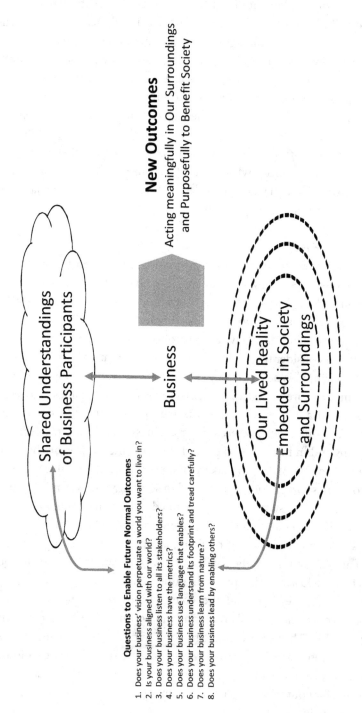

New Outcomes

Acting meaningfully in Our Surroundings and Purposefully to Benefit Society

Shared Understandings of Business Participants

Business

Our Lived Reality Embedded in Society and Surroundings

Questions to Enable Future Normal Outcomes

1. Does your business' vision perpetuate a world you want to live in?
2. Is your business aligned with our world?
3. Does your business listen to all its stakeholders?
4. Does your business have the metrics?
5. Does your business use language that enables?
6. Does your business understand its footprint and tread carefully?
7. Does your business learn from nature?
8. Does your business lead by enabling others?

Figure 12.1 Two anchors for a Future Normal business

with due acknowledgment of our lived reality. Whereas if it continues to operate as if it is in a money-only dreamscape, it will perpetuate patterns that create significant challenges for those who come after us.

This said, we recognize that not every business will make the shift, especially because not all those entrenched in convention are going to suddenly see the light; and as per the argument, change takes time "... opponents eventually die, and a new generation grows up".[2] Hence change can take generations and, in this vein, the challenges of climate change, biodiversity loss and inequality are challenges of generations, especially the generations who will lead after us who are clear they want action on such issues. Hence can today's leaders act or will the challenge be passed over to the next generation?

MAKING THE MOVE

Making the move begins with a conversation and, given the nature of the questions, those conversations may not always be easy. The biggest issue you will face is challenging convention as you will be asking people to consider new possibilities. People are generally resistant to change, hence you will likely face a strong desire to regress to the *now normal*. If you consider the likely conversations, you can probably imagine someone saying: "What have they [the leadership] come up with now?" Such comments are to be expected, change is not a frictionless process.

It is important to remember to pursue purposeful incrementalism with meaningful targets, wherein your business makes a start, celebrates small wins and in turn persists towards its outcomes, especially because the transformation will likely take years, not weeks or months. You will need to think short and long-term, and in so doing you will need to put the change you are starting as one centered within all stakeholders, not just yourself. As such, consider the change as one where the aim is to create a movement that is led by many, as opposed to it being one led by you alone. You may be the spark, but always try and build the change through an inclusive all-in approach, rather than top-down directives.

Beyond the questions and the conversations that they will set in motion, two additional tools that can help you make a start are shown in Figure 12.2. These are conceptual tools and like all such tools they are not absolute, rather they are a way of starting further conversations, a leaping off rather than an end point. The matrices have similar axes, except one is about exploring the footprint of the business and the other benefits to society.

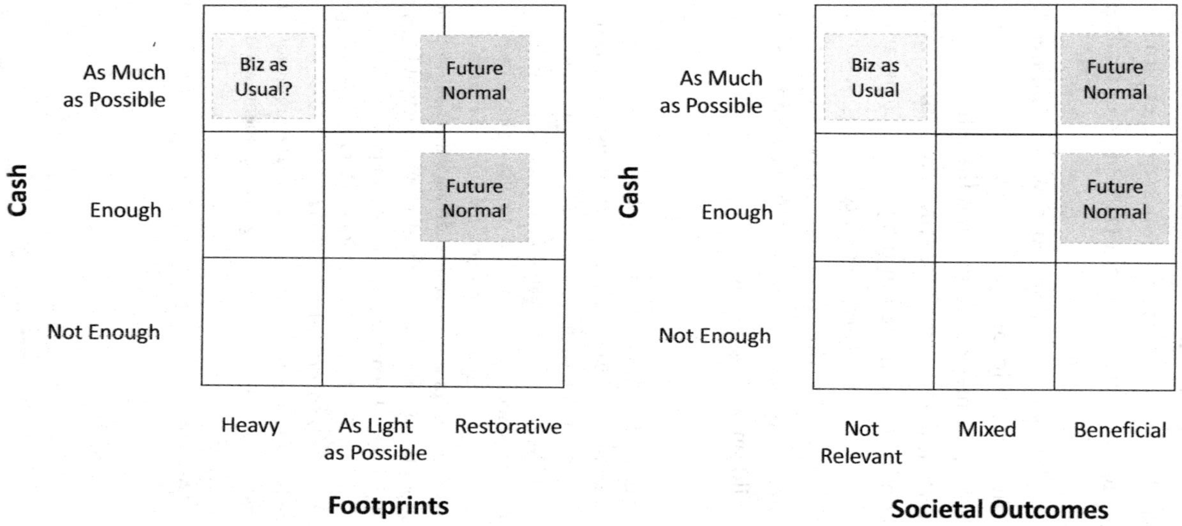

Figure 12.2 Matrices to help you consider your Future Normal

Adapted from Barter, N., & Bebbington, J. (2009). Pursuing Environmental Sustainability. ACCA Global Research Report 116. Available at: https://www.accaglobal.com/content/dam/acca/global/PDF-technical/sustainability-reporting/rr-116-001.pdf

In applying each matrix, plot where your business currently is and then explore where it could be. As you use the tool, you will see that the vertical axis is labelled cash, not profit. This is purposeful; profits are malleable to accounting conventions and the key with any business is to be cashflow positive. As you use the tools you should explore different positions on the matrices and what it might take for your business to be in any one square.

To close, we hope this book has revealed new possibilities for your business. We have tried to reinforce that businesses are not static self-contained things. Rather, businesses are acts and thus the term 'business' should really be a verb. You and your colleagues are acting the business every day, you are continually engaged in the process of organizing and in so doing you are the business. The job of organizing never stops and as such you need to ensure that the conversations continue. So, what to do now? Start the conversation and remember the end game is a business that you and your children will be proud of.

NOTES

1 Lyn Stout, former Distinguished Professor of Corporate and Business Law at the Cornell Law School, describes in a 2012 article how questions regarding the purpose of the corporation during the 1930s led to what is sometimes called the Great Debate, wherein Adolph Berle and Merrick Dodd squared off in the pages of *Harvard Law Review*, with Berle arguing for shareholder primacy and Dodd supporting a broader purpose that includes secure employment, quality products for customers and contributions to the good of society. Stout argues that for several decades that followed the balance was towards corporations being run for all stakeholders and society at large, with that balance shifting again when the Friedman doctrine rose to prominence in the 1970s. See: Stout, L.A. (2012). New Thinking on 'Shareholder Primacy'. *Accounting, Economics, and Law*, 2(2), article 4. https://doi.org/10.1515/2152-2820.1037.

2 This quote is cited as being by the physicist Max Planck. The argument inherent to the quote is reinforced by Thomas Kuhn regarding his arguments about paradigms in science and how they change. These arguments can be found in Khun's book *The Structure of Scientific Revolutions*, originally published by University of Chicago Press in 1962.

Times change and what was innovative becomes normal and what was normal becomes old. Theories and behaviors of the past are not appropriate for our current context, a new approach is needed. This book is underpinned by three big ideas. First, that the questions we ask, and how we ask them, matters. Second, that businesses are the tools we use to shape society and our surroundings. Third, that business value is optimized when society thrives. Thus, the meta-message of this book is that it is time to have the conversations that shift businesses towards operating in a manner that creates long term value for all their stakeholders.

This is easily said but harder to do in practice, not least because we must imagine new possibilities. While we have outlined throughout the book the possibilities afforded through questions and curiosity, there is always a need for someone to show the way and take the first step, that others might follow and enhance. In our experience, this first step, this first conversation is reliant on those who are more playful, who embrace the possible rather than feeling constrained and weighed down by the limits of normality. There is no reason that person cannot be you.

Building on this, we should acknowledge one individual who helped nudge us and his company, Gilbert Guaring, Global Head of Marketing, Sustainability and Engagement for UAP. Every business needs a Gilbert, someone who will start the conversation, encourage colleagues to participate and drive their business towards its Future Normal. To close, having recently spent some time with Gilbert and his colleagues on scoping out the next set of initiatives, a poem arose, that perhaps captures the aesthetic of all that we are trying to enable.

A sapphire dimmed for dreams above
Green for green, for dreams above
Health for wealth, for dreams above

Us for you, for dreams above
When to brighten our sapphire?

Green for green
Wealth for well-being
A much bigger dream
For all our dreams above?
 Nick Barter, March 2023

Printed in the United States
by Baker & Taylor Publisher Services